knucklebones

sam hunt
knucklebones
POEMS 1962–2012

craig potton publishing

Published in 2012 by Craig Potton Publishing

Craig Potton Publishing
98 Vickerman Street, PO Box 555, Nelson, New Zealand
www.craigpotton.co.nz

Poems © Sam Hunt

ISBN 978-1-877517-71-6

Printed in China by Everbest Printing Ltd

This book is copyright. Apart from any fair dealing for the purposes of private study, research, criticism or review, as permitted under the Copyright Act, no part may be reproduced by any process without the permission of the publishers.

CONTENTS

Christmas 1953 14

PREFACE
BRACKEN COUNTRY

Beware the man 18
Walking the morning city 19
Post Office report 20
A house north near mangroves 21
August steam 22
A wind of wolves 23
Collision 24
A Mangaweka road song 25
School policy on stickmen 26
Bracken country 27

FROM BOTTLE CREEK

We could just disappear 30
Letter home 31
Flutemaker 32
My white ship 33
Homecoming 34
Invocation in Equinox 36
Singing for you now 37
Plea before storm 38
At Castor Bay 39
A white gentian 40
A song about her 41

July 21 1969	42
Somewhere near here; many miles	43
Porirua Friday night	44
A summer poem	45
A Bottle Creek blues	46
A hot-water bottle baby blues	47
My father scything	48
Return in spring	49
Postcard of a cabbage tree	50
Before the demolitions	52
Smash	53
Her words on leaving	54
A school report	55
Saturday Palm Sunday	56
A valley called Moonshine	57
Four bow-bow poems	58
A purple balloon	60
Photograph of Robin in war-paint	62

SOUTH INTO WINTER

The windows of our morning	66
A long time	67
Himatangi	68
Stabat Mater	69
Early opener	70
Notes from a journey	72
Just like that!	73
Modigliani girl	74
Lyn	75
Four cobweb poems	76

Road song Paekakariki 78
After sickness 80

TIME TO RIDE

Time to ride 84
Your ultimate accountant 85
Black cattle at dawn, Waiura 86
Christina 88
You house the moon 89
Maintrunk country road song 90
Every time it rains like this 91
Of Dan and the Peacock 92

DRUNKARD'S GARDEN

Drunkard's garden 96
Friend to many 97
Two winter settings 98
Ana gathering cones on Battle Hill 99
Girl with black eye in grocer's shop 100
Words on a first waking 101
Four songs 102
Those eyes; such mist 104
No Exit 105
Birth of a son 106
Wagoning, up Moonshine 107
Baptism by river water 108
For Kristin and Tom on a stormy morning 109
The men of Moonshine 110
My father today 111

Liz 112
Up Battle Hill 113

COLLECTED POEMS

Rainbows, and a promise of snow 116
Hilary 118
Four Manly verses 120
Salt man 121
Sailor's morning 122
Return to Drunken Bay 124
Return to Rangitoto 125
Song for Tom 126
West Coast woman 127
Death of the poet preacherman 128
April Fool 129
River woman songs 130
Requiem 132

RUNNING SCARED

Running scared 136
After separation 138
Beyond the brink 140
Words for Tina 141
Brother Lynch 142
Passing through 145
Returned Serviceman 146
Ancient taupata, Bottle Creek 148
Death in the street 150
Bottle to Battle to Death 152
Dead bird 154
New words 157

APPROACHES TO PAREMATA

October in the bay	160
Patea 1983	162
Arthur Allan Thomas	164
Wedding party and after	165
Six summer sestets	166
Lisa from Manjimup	168
Wave song	169

SELECTED POEMS

We are nearly neighbours	172
Waikato river song	173
Glimpse	174
Hitting 40	175

ANGEL GEAR

I wonder what the old man is thinking?	178
Foreign hotel	179
Making tracks	180
Spider song	182
The man on the sandtrack said	183
Tora wind song	184
What dandelions think	185
Yellow	186
Bone flute	187
September 1st	188
Clearing the ashes out	190
Oterei rivermouth	191
Catching the tide	192
Not in this weather	193

Rangitaiki road song 194
Four plateau songs 196
Sara 198

MAKING TRACKS

Coming to it 202
Seven years 203
It's rain today in Sydney 204
After words 205
That feeling-of-being-in-the-country 206
War history 207
Rangitikei river song 208

DOWN THE BACKBONE

A new plateau song 212
Why a man 213
Fire, as always 214
Old flames 215
Hey, Minstrel 216
Working the Genesis week 218
Making it back in 219
Harpooner's song 220
Floating poem 222
Fucking poem 223
There isn't a river 224
That's it 225
Naming the Gods 226

DOUBTLESS

Doubtless 230
Arapaoa 249

Tree poem	250
He was one of the last	251
Normal enough	252
Missing you	254
Snap/shot	256
As we speak	257
Whose turn is it?	258
Poem on Meg's death	259
I throw you flowers	260
Patron Saint song	261
Sunset song	262
No bells	264
What takes your fancy	266
Cloud song	267
Jimmy Vernon	268
Better than this?	269
Sonata	270
Lugging the sack	272
Lines for a New Year	274
Talking of the weather	280

CHORDS

Chord 1	284
Chord 2	285
Chord 3	286
Chord 4	286
Chord 5	287
Chord 6	287
Chord 7	288
Chord 8	289
Chord 9	290

Janáček chord	291
Chord 11	292
Chord 12	294
Chord 13	295
Chord 14	296
Chord 15	297
Chord 16	298
Chord 17	300
Chord 18	301
Boathouse chord	302
Chord 20	303
Chord 21	303
Chord 22	304
Chord 23	305
Chord 24	306
Chord 25	307
Chord 26	308
Chord 27	309
Chord 28	310
Chord 29	311
Chord 30	312
Chord 31	313
Chord 32	314
Chord 33	315
Chord 34	316
Tokatoka chord	317
Chord 36	318
Chord 37	320
Chord 38	321
Chord 39	322
Chord 40	323

Chord 41	324
Chord 42	325
All weathers chord	326
Raupo chord	327
The Loki chords	330
Rain! but not enough	332
A long summer	333
Blessed the fruit	334
Blackbird song	336
11 Runes (for Alf, turning 11)	337
It was the old story	340
Diana	341
It's all okay	342
Move on song	344
Not these days	345
They are clouds	346
To a sparrow	347
To be a house	348
Looking for the lights	350
Death notices	351
Last in line	352

KNUCKLEBONES

Five knucklebones	356

Christmas 1953

Climb up the cliff path to
the pines where through
their needles salt winds blow

and far below
the fish and ocean go

and down the cliff path home
bring a lone
Christmas tree

and by the beach
let it in warm winds grow.

    (Sam Hunt, age 7)

PREFACE

Knucklebones is a collection of poems selected from all Sam Hunt's published work. While this book begins with poems from *Bracken Country*, his first collection published in 1971, this collection actually spans 50 years of writing, as the earliest poem in this collection was written in 1962, before concluding with poems written in 2012. The only one of Sam's books not drawn from in *Knucklebones* is the autobiographical *Backroads: Charting a Poet's Life* (Craig Potton Publishing, 2009).

A chronological outrider in this collection is *Christmas 1953*, the poem facing this preface. While Sam has always remembered this poem (his recall for thousands of poems is legendary), it was not until after his mother's death, while sorting through her papers, that he found a definitive hard copy. It was written at his childhood home at Milford Beach on the North Shore of Auckland, at the age of seven. The poems have not stopped since.

BRACKEN COUNTRY
1971

Beware the man

Beware the man who tries to fit you out
In his idea of a hat
Dictating the colour and the shape of it.

He takes your head and carefully measures it
Says 'Of course black's out'.
He sees himself in the big black hat.

So you may be a member of the act
He makes for you your special coloured hat.
Beware! He's fitting you for more than that.

Walking the morning city

Walking the morning city
the opposite direction
workers walking toward me
walking from the sun:
I have no job to go to
so walk into the station

watch the all-night Limited
pull in at the platform
pretend I'm waiting for
a friend who never came:
pretend I'm disappointed
vamp my blues harmonica

buy a lightweight pad
and biro at the station store
coffee at the cafeteria
pretend to write a letter:
have no one to write to
so drink a cup and leave

walk down morning streets
lightweight in the sun
no one to tell this to
'cause no one is my lover.
This morning more than ever
I'm set on finding you.

Post Office report

'No space for human error,'
the postmaster tells me,
'they're a team my workers here.'

Morning tea-break I meet the team:
efficient, incredibly
ugly every one of them.

Understaffed? in need maybe
of extra office space? I suggest
an arm-chair for pension day.

My report goes on, every
date-stamp initialled and timed –
surprised I'm not asked to stay!

'We're running an office here,'
he tells me, 'not a home' –
looking to his nodding team.

My report is official,
complete by noon. But I stay, all
day: they think I'll never go.

I won't. I'm waiting for the one
human error these P.O.
workers never counted on.

A house north near mangroves

You rarely see your face at
moments now that matter much.
It's when, say, shaving – and that's
once in a month at a stretch;
or tying a tie, adjusting
the noose for easy breathing.

How many, hearing the news
their grandfather died last night
in a house north near mangroves –
too far from where you are right
then at the moment you're told;
too late – how many have held
their face to a mirror that
moment? watched it in the wide
mirror above the driver's seat.

Instead of school as usual,
you are dressed up one morning,
bundled with fat sacks of mail
aboard a bus with your mother.
After you're sick of watching
cows watching each other,
you ask her *Where are we going?*
'Your grandfather. He died last
night.' And watch your mouth twist

to a great big question-mark.
You try twisting it further
over the driver's shoulder
till it makes you laugh. You ask
her again and keep watching
your face. *Mum where are we going?*

August steam

The lake made no sense early on:
driving down a slipway straight
two truant kids in a big V8
parking in a rain storm
huddled in beside the lake.

It made no sense then early on:
it wasn't till much later
we understood things better
nothing could go wrong –
you said let's drive forever.

We could only return:
the sulphur city drenched
steaming after rain: so ditched
the faithful love machine
made in for a dressing shed.

Undressed each other in turn:
I never thought I'd ever
be your winter hot-pool lover
until I was right then.
Some things are never over.

A wind of wolves

The first page of *Zhivago*
the boy is on a mound of clay
beside his mother's grave.
My friend's funeral today,

already rain
at 5 a.m. An upstairs guest,
I hear a wind of wolves,
no flowers by request.

Collision

I took the punch like glass.
I didn't break, I shattered.
A car smash once, head on.

One day I started reading poems
where people said they looked out
crying through their tears –

I believe in all these things –
like looking at you dead
through shattered glass.

A Mangaweka road song

No place more I'd like to bring you than
this one-pub town
approached in low gear down
the gorges through the hills.

Now they've built the by-pass
the drinkers left are locals
and odd commercial travellers.
Quiet afternoons like this you hear the falls.

On the Post Office corner
a blue flag floats. I bought
a hot meat pie at the store,
a new harmonica.

A public bar drinker
tells me what I want to hear.
I play for him later
songs on my harmonica.

We know each other now.
I buy my round of beers,
I catch up on the news
in small town public bars.

They ask me why I travel
and never settle down.
I lose two games of pool
and hitch-hike out of town.

School policy on stickmen

It's said that children should not use
stick figures when they draw.
And yet I've lain all night awake
looking at this drawing here
of orange men, stick figures every one of them,
walking up a crayon mountain hand in hand
walking up my wall.

They're edging up a ridge
their backs against the mountain
pinned against my wall.
And every one is smiling.
They know the way a mountain laughs,
especially crayon mountains made of brown.
They know they're not allowed,
these orange men.

Bracken country

Walk the wagon line
Embankments either side,
A half full flagon, harsh dry wine,
Underneath your arm.

The folks back home
Call you by your name.
Walk, son, drink, speak well of every
Single one of them.

FROM BOTTLE CREEK
1972

We could just disappear

We disappear,
ten carriages of us,
a tunnel as long as
tomorrow, next term,
a tunnel as long as next year,
as long as time.

No one knows when
we will come out the other end –
we could go on and on and
on forever and never
come out again.
We could just disappear.

Letter home

When things get too hard to bear
row out and catch the tide,
our blue dinghy stacked with beer;
ride the drift whichever way
as long as that long tide and half
the cold brown bottles last;
don't fear you'll ever be lost.

And if by the end of today
you catch the turned tide, love,
you'll be home, back in our bay,
the two black cats catching sprats,
gulls scavenging for the catch,
at the end of the first day
since they sent me away.

Flutemaker
(a lament)

More regular than clockwork,
the sad retired captain down
the dune path would hobble for
sands where all night oceans break,
and with the sunlight roam,
dazed, the orphanage of the shore.

Poised like day he would then scan
forms abandoned by surf the
night before... gnomons now on
a sun-struck dial of shore;
and like the day, move through the
arc traced out by the flotsam.

Many white years later, late
one evening, the bent captain
found the form he'd searched so long
from which he would carve a flute;
marry his dry silences,
age and frailty, in song.

Up in his shack on the dunes
he chiselled all through the night,
until when day broke he knew
his brittle labour was done:
so the captain pursing tight
dry lips, down the white shaft blew.

And dark, giving itself up
in long slivers to distilled
shrill white shafts of morning sun,
left sunlight dancing on the
bent shadow of a crippled
captain whistling on the dunes.

My white ship

Although together we
Drift the bay's slow pull
Of tides and know this sea
Behind the island will
Never drag us away,
And drifting lift not one
White sail to trap the day
Nor catch the sun,

The ethic of my love
For you remains that I
Am a lone sailor of
The night; captain of my
White ship: and though you be
A good day's mate, your fight's
Too weak to ride with me
These wild black nights.

So lie please in the peace of
Your anchored sleep, and do
Not cry for help, my love,
As if I'm drowning you,
But lie on without fright
When I raise my sail up
And ride out on the night
On my white ship.

Homecoming

1 'Rainy Day Woman'

The woman you made me is
copper, coal, beads and painted glass,
hung high, a world of colour
in my universe of rain.

She is, while you're away,
my woman for a rainy day.

Each morning I plait her wire
the golden copper of her hair,
then hang her from the rafters
so she knows the day is hers.

She watches like a cynic
as I knock the whiskies back –
until the final drink is done
when I curse that I was born,
and blame my drunken stupor on
the sadness in the falling rain...

and I watch my coal-and-beaded
copper-haired and painted bride

let her cynic's look fall down
and turn her colours in the rain.

2 *The Bay*

Last night the world was as black
as the black shag on the rock,

but now the morning has come
and tomorrow you come home;

my 'Rainy Day Woman' waits...

Yes, this morning with a new
sun spinning white on the blue

even the giant shag sits,
black wings tilted like kites:

and as heat from sunlight throbs
through the stirring bay, salt globes

of water bristle like sweat
on its outstretched wings. We wait.

The black shag splinters the light.

Invocation in Equinox

Ozone floats for days, sweet and
heavy on the heaving wind:

all along the beach, washed-up
logs will lie like us asleep.

This is how it always is
this time of year, always,

every March, the equinox
brings storm: as now: black winds knock

at the rusty French doors till
you're sure Death has come to call...

But forget your fears. I, too,
cannot sleep tonight although

I've been through many storms. Do
not worry, please... Tomorrow

morning I'll take you for a
short walk round our yawn of bay

and let you, child, roam the shore –
you'll find there's nothing to fear;

then lead you slowly home, up
past the heaving logs to sleep.

Singing for you now

I'd rambled on, uncertain of
My songs, vague memories of love,
    Sung them two years now,
When really knowing nothing more
Than empty bottles round the floor;
    Waking, doomed, at noon.

But then two months ago you came
Bringing me your childlike calm,
    Something wholly new –
To wake up with the first light breaking
Through your dark, lashed eyes; and making
    Love, not song, to you.

    And now I gather you
Dry firewood and flowers from the cliff,
And lastly this, this song plucked live
    From silence, love,

    Singing for you now.

Plea before storm

Like the sky-high seagulls
tossed from those thundering black
boulders of the clouds, you are
girl, setting off back home,
looking for the things you've lost –
a mislaid purse and raincoat,
wondering where you put them last;
and nearly ready now to climb
the cliffpath, trying to recall
the home you left for this,
what way you came.

The macrocarpa blackness
quickens; pine-belts black on the hills.

Storm is coming in that crazed
rustle of leaves, the frenzied
laughter of the seagulls skidding
spread-eagled on the light. Like ice
setting, the light sets hard.

It is coming fast. Lightning
and thunder quicken. No pause.

I'm sorry, forget what I said.
Come back inside.

At Castor Bay

I found the colour of your
flesh again this morning:
a tidal bank exposed
at dead low water, shells
the colour of your flesh.

This coast again... sun rising
over islands this blue May
morning reefed inside the bay
where sunlight floods:
wading to my knees, fat
black seagulls on the smooth hard sand
and water clapping, the rock-pools
drained... familiar
but no less bright,
your silken crevices.

A white gentian

Remember Ruapehu,
that mountain, six months ago?
You sat in an alpine hut
sketching scoria, red
rusted outcrops in the snow.

I climbed some southern peak
and made up the sort of song
men climbing mountains sing:
how, no longer your lover,
I knew it was over.

I thought I'd try out my song
when I returned that evening
as though there were nothing wrong.
Instead I brought a flower down
smelling of the mountain.

A song about her

My liquor bill cut by half
up from two years with the dead
I've ripped my faded pin-ups down
kicked my pillows out of bed.

Trotting her home last night
down past Mount Street Cemetery
my silent girl she said how much
she hoped she'd soon see more of me.

Then as yesterday at Makara Beach
I did not try the ancient move
for fear I would destroy
what only time and silence do.

Two years out of practice
writing cool Platonic songs about
a girl too innocent to seize
the hot rod of a V8 lout,

I'm singing now because the shellbanks
shine and in the sun here, sober,
smoking her last night's butts,
I know I love her.

July 21 1969

I read you an angry man's
       poem of war-time in Milan,
1944... Two years
       you say, before we were born
and this went on, it's crazy!
       (A rock star died last month. Two men
this morning walked on the moon.)

Nothing shocks anyone now...
       when I read of Jones's death
it should have been as impersonal
       as that bathroom in the station.
But it stunned me somehow –
       as if, with a tap on the door,
I'd been joined by the queer custodian.

I know many our age have died
       but when by suicide
it's something more than death.
       The bathroom roared like an oven.
I coughed steam. Clenched my eyes to it.
       Nothing shocks anyone, even
men on the moon. I like the old poems.

Somewhere near here; many miles

Somewhere near here, many miles,
this night of rain is falling
hard on corrugated iron
inlet shacks. Here, soft on tiles;

and if the door weren't open
it may just as well be yet
another comfortable night,
the electric blanket on...

the rain hitting down hard while
this State suburb sleeps: you would
hardly know... another world
somewhere near here; many miles.

Porirua

Porirua Friday night

Acne blossoms scarlet on their cheeks,
These kids up Porirua East...
Pinned across this young girl's breast
A name-tag on the supermarket badge;
A city-sky-blue smock.
Her face unclenches like a fist.

Fourteen when I met her first
A year ago, she's now left school,
Going with the boy
She hopes will marry her next year.
I asked if she found it hard
Working in the store these Friday nights
When friends are on the town.

        She never heard:
But went on, rather, talking of
The house her man had put
A first deposit on
And what it's like to be in love.

A summer poem

We would never build our huts
in macrocarpa trees:
the brooding darkness, wetness,
in darker greenness was
where wetas and those birds
that peck your eyes out lived.

Sun and the smell of the gum,
we built instead in the pines,
hoisting with ropes limb to limb
planks from the timber yard;
and other days we would use
the ropes as swings…

A friend once swung to a roar
some forty feet up –
the highest that summer –
the rope tied to nothing more
than a peg of a limb.
The whole next week he was King.

A Bottle Creek blues

The wind can't blow any harder,
the air's as heavy as Hell...

I watched blue diesel smoke like mist
hanging on a high suburban hill:
wind I thought would blow it away
but the wind itself is diesel.

And yet the smoke disappeared
absorbed by that suburban hill:
the problem of disposal was
solved by the lungs of the people.

Two years ago we used to row
to an island here called Cockleshell:
gather cockles in a sack,
warm them up and gorge ourselves.

A friend I used to do this with
near died from typhoid fever:
they had the cockles analysed –
shit from down the coastline further.

Barefeet on the beach is madness,
this beach that was once made of sand:
sun shines bright on broken glass,
cockles from Cockleshell Island are banned.

Sad protest songs are sung and heard
like this one here. And afterwards
the audience goes home convinced
the shit's cleared clean away with words...

The wind can't blow any harder,
the air's too heavy for the birds.

A hot-water bottle baby blues

All that I love alive I've killed,
nothing to save, still less to lose:
these nights I suffer from the cold
hot-water bottle baby blues.

An afternoon I left you tucked
trembling like a rain-downed bird
beneath a bank, and three times tacked
my way upstream, but soon was bored.

I raced a log back down the stream
until, still underneath the bank,
I found you crouched. It was no dream.
You asked me for a piggyback.

Clutching lightly as a bird,
warm heart beating on my back, you grinned,
waving your arms round as I bowed –
and just like that we left the ground.

We flew all night until I could
fly no more... and falling, felt you lose
your warmth... I woke up with the cold
hot-water bottle baby blues.

My father scything

My father was sixty when I was born,
twice my mother's age. But he's never been
around very much, neither at the mast
round the world; nor when I wanted him most.
He was somewhere else, like in his upstairs
Dickens-like law office counting the stars;
or sometimes out with his scythe on Sunday
working the path through lupin toward the sea.

And the photograph album I bought myself
on leaving home, lies open on the shelf
at the one photograph I have of him,
my father scything. In the same album
beside him, one of my mother.
I stuck them there on the page together.

Return in spring

1

At war all day in the buffalo grass,
Our backs would itch all night. And each tall pine,
Five of them, stirred as if by sea-winds in the mind;
Raw smell of gum where we'd hammered nails in.

Tree-huts in their limbs: mine, the last one down
The section from the house. Once a summer bach
This place, sprawled over the years, room on room,
Like lupin down the run-down garden to the beach.

2

I have no memories as others do
Of family outings: we had it all here,
White sand, ocean, Wairau Creek and bridge,
The orchard where we laid our bodies bare.

The lupin too, a lattice-work of dens
Deep in foliage... down a corridor
Of green October light, a small boy knocked
His first girl up, shoving through her bolted door.

3

I took all this this morning, piece by piece,
And nothing seemed the same. The corridors
Through lupin and down the pine tree limbs
Were splayed; and where were huts and dens, claws.

Only later, when I had been along the beach
And seen again the orchard, bridge and creek,
Could I recall each hut, and find that still
The pine trees bleed where once our nails struck.

Postcard of a cabbage tree

1

Pith where a hard heart should be.
Climb but never hope to find
Anything but blossoms for a mind.
I'm more a lily than a tree.

And ignore the picture please.
I'm not what it makes out I am.
Just rip it up and call me Sam,
An old flat-footed cabbage tree.

2

Few believe in what they see.
Your friends prefer to call it myth
Passed down by drunken word of mouth:
They say such things just cannot be,

That in the spring a heavy
Blossom forecasts summer drought.
Forget them please, don't ever doubt
An old flat-footed cabbage tree.

3

And don't come here to study.
These brackish winds up Bottle Creek
Would make the best mind crack.
It's safer in some library.

Come rather for the early
Mornings waking in the bach,
At the south end of the beach
An old flat-footed cabbage tree.

4
And please don't probe the heart in me
Initialling your own
Name deep into my bone.
You'll end up on your knees

Wondering how you let this be-
Come the tombstone of our love,
Knelt at the knotted ankles of
An old flat-footed cabbage tree.

5
And so to ramble on all night.
So easy, finding images
Of proper postcard size.
But none of them are right.

I'm nothing more than what you see…
At my feet, Pied Piper boots
Standing where I must collapse,
An old flat-footed cabbage tree.

Before the demolitions
(for Janet)

A groper boat has just tied up, fresh
from days in the Straits. They unload their fish.
And a woman in a small bikini
catches herrings in a jar... Here the sea
joins hands, the tides do whirlpools;
tin shacks squat on piles
between State Highway One and
the railway bridge... you came in the end

in love or out of love. But a barge
is tethered today by the bridge,
a railway gang with chainsaws there.
They lay new jarra sleepers. And some other
day soon, some gang will bulldoze us out.
Until then we learn to love by heart.

Slug Alley

Smash
(for Meg)

Moths on the farmhouse window
batter like rain on the glass:
they're allowed a half-inch gap
where I left the door ajar.

I have sat here hours watching.
And now at last one's made it,
a dizzy lady off course.
She flutters on white-hot light.

And still on the window-pane
a million more moths outside…
Watch them skid! how they collide
and trickle down with the rain.

Her words on leaving

I began to wake in suburbs
padding cold concrete for
a four-bottle plastic crate.
The last house in the street.

Wrought iron hedges the garden.
It keeps the hill from rolling
flat and away, our unborn
children in…

The man at the hospital
said Drink lots of milk.
I woke up a long time later,
a cap of curlers for hair.

But I soon have to leave…
People always told me
Travel while you can, you're young.
I've travelled all my life.

I'm not sick. But I hate,
fear more than your coming, the grate
of tubular steel on iron,
the click of the gate.

A school report

Working with these young kids in the pastel
clay frontier, we live near bulldozer blades.
The school I came to yesterday had loads
of children waiting: that was all.
The road up the valley still a shingle path.
The town planners never predicted such birth.

They write short poems, the kids. 'I wish I was rich I
wish I had gold wings I am made out of sky…'
They paint houses pastel, and the houses
smudge. I told them this morning how wild horses
and moonshiners lived here once. Late on today
a group of them made a model city of clay.

Saturday Palm Sunday

I live on a long inlet
often write down lines about it
songs that people living in
the suburbs and the cities sing.

This morning when I rowed across
the channel to the bottle store
two pied oystercatchers were
padding on a mudbank.

This afternoon with a shy friend,
cold beer on the jetty,
talk about the week just over
and how the oystercatcher feeds;

drive up Moonshine later on,
drink more, a harsh home wine,
cook sausages and know you're gone,
no reason now to write songs down.

A valley called Moonshine

The lights in the farmhouses
go out. The inlet is out.

An iron shack on the shoreline
floats its light on the water.

A grandfather up Moonshine
remembers the first daughter.

Dreams are easy. Wild horses.

Four bow-bow poems

1

You woke my mother up this morning
At six o'clock with your barking

So she took away your barks
And put them in the bow-wow box

She tied you up she took your barks away
Now all you do is smile at strangers all day

You aren't a guard dog anymore
You aren't even a dog anymore!

2

I don't really think I like
A dog that can't bark when he likes

So all by myself this afternoon
I took the bow-wow box down

It was hidden in behind a lot of books
And I gave you back eleven big barks

You've run outside to use them up
I think you've woken the baby up!

3
Look, here are some simple facts:
You'll find in the poetry books
One thousand and twelve poems about cats

There are all sorts of poems about cats
Cats chasing rats, cats wearing hats,
Cats that simply sit on mats

But you look for bow-wow poetry
And it's quite a different story.
Right now there are only three.

And one more makes four . . .

They often ask me why
I write this bow-wow poetry

I'll tell you
And cross-my-heart it's true

I've got nothing else to do.

A *purple balloon*

1

As father to five children
they say he failed. His drinking
whisky for a week non-stop,
at every gulp, blinking,
at the wonder of it all,
the same blue eyes my mother
sometimes says she sees in me.
My grandfather was, they say,
a failure of the first degree.

And every Christmas Day, our
drunk old Santa Claus, he came.
With a pohutukawa
flower stuck like a clotted bloom
of blood on his coat lapel:
pockets full: always his green
bottle with its latch-on cap;
singing with us kids till all
we could do was yell and clap...

The last Christmas he came he
gave me a purple balloon.

Just turned twelve, I hitch-hiked
north to Waiotu: run-down
farms and eroded hills; clay,
skylines gaping red with clay;
spending Easter with him in
his shack of fibrolite and tin:
for the three days drinking wine
he'd crushed from grape and let
ferment in an old tin can...

Hangover sun and Sunday,
songs and a purple balloon.

2

When gangrene set in, my
grandfather's feet on a rack,
laid in a hospital bed
he watched them slowly turn black.
But even after they'd cut
both his legs to the knee, still
he claimed he could twitch his toes
and would ask for flowers at night
and what they'd done with his shoes.

Waiting the priest, no one
seemed to know quite what to do.
My mother watched the empty pit.
Hands behind their backs, the grave-
diggers wore white denim coats.
And after the priest had come
and gone, and the white men slid
the coffin down, we all dropped
paper poppies on the lid…

I tried to believe but couldn't
forget the purple balloon.

Drinking all day in this far
north harbour pub, I couldn't
help think of him, now dead. With
salt and whisky on his breath,
some sand-barred sailor locals
here still talk about, who stalks
the sand-bar singing where he
drowned one night: drunk, rolling
drunk on whisky down the bar…

I couldn't help think of his
night; and a purple balloon.

Photograph of Robin in war-paint

Those big eyes they are like black
stones emerging through the snow.
Spring has made the mountains cry,
the whites of your wide eyes thaw...

Come on, no tears now!

I have seen you often, mouth
puckered and your hair undone.
Even war-paint on your face
won't frighten me, dear Indian:

I have so often watched you
painting it all on, and know
the cheeky girl who tries to
startle adults with a show.

But they are not interested.
They've already decided
long-haired cowboys should be scalped
and pretty Indians shot dead...

Come on, off to bed.

SOUTH INTO WINTER
1973

The windows of our morning

The mists descend again – no
plate-glass hillside view today

You wake in tears – no
recriminations now

> *that's all over*
> *be my love or*
> *show me the door*

I've said it all before – no
recriminations now

> *I love ya (yip!)*
> *w' all m' heart*
> *an' y' know it*

The mists a long time ago
surrounded us

The windows of our morning
burst into light; into tears

A long time

A long time now and everyone
let us know what they think best,
tells us what we should have done –
stay together, love; or bust.

We're given final warning
today after a long time talking;
and in the mist of the morning
my love and I go walking.

Himatangi

When Leo died, his widow Mrs Sim
kept the corner wine-stop running; the roadside
macrocarpa hedge neatly trimmed as ever

W-I-N-E it is clipped to spell. Make time, stop there,
vineyard prices (cutting government tax).
She's housed men on the run since World War One

Inside the house, photographs in sepia:
Leo; Lenin; dead comrades round the walls;
play the player piano; plan the Revolution

A little lady giving the Red Guard sign
(the right fist raised), she showed me the moon,
'There's a hammer and a sickle up there too!'

Mrs Sim, because of you the moon
will always be a sickle; the hammer
raised, the ceaseless beating heart of a man

Stabat Mater

My mother called my father 'Mr Hunt'
For the first few years of married life.
I learned this from a book she had inscribed:
'To dear Mr Hunt, from his loving wife.'

She was embarrassed when I asked her why
But later on explained how hard it had been
To call him any other name at first, when he –
Her father's elder – made her seem so small.

Now in a different way, still like a girl,
She calls my father every other sort of name;
And guiding him as he roams old age
Sometimes turns to me as if it were a game…

That once I stand up straight, I too must learn
To walk away and know there's no return.

Early opener

> Why stay sober when
> all the weatherman
> predicts is rain

Belfast, Dublin, Cork... no big bomb scares here
up Molesworth Street, the Hotel Wellington,
 an early opener;
the last before a man clears clean out of town

A 15-stoner rises from his chair
already pissed and dancing queer:
 a day on full pay,
the wharves closed down for wet weather

A long-bar heater just above head height
burns your eyes until they smart,
 your forehead sweat,
makes your heartbeat rise like vomit

In walks the regular-most-regular,
bulldog 'Champ' with overshot jaw,
 alcohol and cold;
trembling with the early morning laughter

He sways, lurching under pats, between tables.
We talk all morning of the world and what it
 says in the paper.
'Champ' champs beer from a bowl marked 'Champ'

This morning's *Dominion*, the IRA
made headlines, man: among these latter-day
 New Zealand Irish,
any news is news, news from faraway

And any good moment now, old Brendan himself
breathing heavy from a heavy night before,
    Death himself warmed up!
His dream were words. He clears the upper shelf

The Archangels themselves, I am told,
old Lucifer and all his irate union men,
    argued it out
in this very pub. They complained of the cold

These voices are voices in a sad dream,
faces of last Irish sunset… 'Fed up,
    fucked and far from home';
defrocked bishops, every lone one of them

St Patrick's dead drunk in the Serpent Bar,
'Champ' is asleep, bloated on black 'n' tan:
    this early opener,
her doors wide open to all lost men

    Why stay sober when
    all the weatherman
    predicts is rain

Notes from a journey
(for Hone)

When I left Whanganui
(you and Eve asleep still
low under canvas) my pilgrimage
was northward up
the river of the three taniwha

The sun shone; every little
township had its one-way bridge.
By midday, man, it seemed
a month instead of
half a day since leaving

Three o'clock that afternoon
I picked up three local boys,
Tawe, Gabriel, Andrew;
drove them through
Pipiriki out to Raetihi

They told me of Hemi, how
a month ago he walked
the whole way out on foot
'27 bloody miles of it!'
He died soon after that

'What if we meet old Hemi
around the next bend?' I asked.
'Let the bugger walk it'
one boy laughed. I turned
laughing with him

His face was dust and tears.
I passed him the bottle,
double declutching,
chopping down the gears.
It was a steep, slow climb.

Just like that!

So close, the poisonous berries
so close! Lying where you are
so close, this minute here,
you reach out and pick
a cluster of orange-red berries;
pop them in like jaffas. You
can be a child again, eat
more than's good for you –
here! like this – die
this minute here now where you lie.
One two three, that's it,
just like that!

Modigliani girl
(a faded denim blues)

You came one day
cute little dress
long brown neck
yeah you made me 'come
a nervous wreck

Yeah in you came
drove me mad
my mind aswirl
my mod Modigli-mod
li-ani Girl

Said you'd stay
then yesterday
you went away
left me with the faded
denim blues

Go on take my jeans
walk on down
the pathway home
your little Levi bum
zip still half undone

Denim blues
my mind aswirl
you drive me mad
my mod Modigli-mod
li-ani Girl

Lyn

These are the waking hours, the hours between
two a.m. in winter and the dawn...
Shaken trembling from a dream:
someone screaming: like a baby new born.

The hours closest to death, tumbling in
a darkness darker than the womb or cave.
It is impossible to sleep again,
too many voices: tall Mark; Dave

who never made it in that fat old mother-
fucking Ford V8 past Waiwera: dead
drunk with one hand on the wheel; the other
down some sheila's pants. That's how he died.

Impossible to sleep, too many voices:
Mark is telling someone something: to do
with bikes for sure; his wild horses.
I listen now. You're next, Lyn. I wait for you

and sure enough, you scream!
You're dead. You may as well have not been born...
I find my poems are written down between
two a.m. in winter and the dawn.

Four cobweb poems

1

I've even named him now
this spider on the seaward window of my shack

I've watched him grow
watched him spin his first bright web

And then one day first thing
at six o'clock one early summer morning

I watched my spider catch
his first black fly

2

I feel for him
my spider on the window

Felt nothing for his victim
the fat black blowfly

My spider and I
we feel for each other

Nothing much can ever come between us
That's why I let him have the fly!

3

My spider often used to ask me why
I wrote him cobweb poetry

I told him
I really didn't know

If he wanted answers to questions like that
he'd better go

Spin himself a bigger brighter web
and leave my seaward window

4

And this is now the end
the end of cobweb poems

A girl came to my house last night
spinning faster than a cobwebbed fly she was

She didn't like my kind of home
that was what she said

Then she killed my spider dead
that was what she did…

So this, friends, is the last bright cobweb poem!

Road song Paekakariki

1

A time when many break –
the blue heron stands more
alone than ever before.
I'm on the road again,
a small town public bar,
wondering where they all have gone;

read in tonight's paper
a head-on collision
a mile down Highway One:
the car, a Chevy, ran
right underneath a ten-ton
truck at sixty miles an hour,

no names in the paper,
they still have no idea
who the victims were
or even their sex –
by our mid-twenties
a few have made headlines!

2

A time when many break –
the boys who joined the clubs
the universities
Jaycees and well-paid jobs;
traded in their old V8s
for wheels less expensive –

where do they live?
I can count one or two:
one old friend, she came through,
alone, fighting, alive;
a few men, too. The rest,
they're dead…

the blue heron's more
alone than ever before,
the gulls have all migrated
off to the graveyard;
the second-hand car dealer
buys me a beer.

After sickness
(for Jerry)

Watching you paddling belly down
out on to the Tasman
I thought of an old duck
beating for the air

thought of the grey morning men
the men who come to kill you,

last mad duck of the season

TIME TO RIDE
1975

Time to ride
(The last time I saw Larry happy)

The last time I saw Larry happy
He was driving a Ford V8 truck
Clapping down in top Moonshine Valley:
Thumbed him down, knew I was in luck.

Drove the drunk Horokiris, foot down flat,
A couple of tired old V8 louts
Going thin on top, fast going to fat,
Ten years of heavy drinking bouts.

Larry seemed changed, like he didn't belong,
Seemed like he had nowhere left to drive to:
Something had somewhere gone wrong:
Whatever it was, neither knew.

We drank out that day at the Paekak pub,
Got cornered by some smug suburban fool.
He kept baiting Larry, 'Won't you ever grow up?
You can't spend your life playing pool!'

Larry cracked later. I took it first,
Nothing much more than a mid-twenties menopause,
Nothing much more: never thought it would last;
Never a moment suspected the cause.

Time to ride … I know in a way it was.
Larry's changed, has friends who are witty and waspy.
Larry's changed, will never be like he was
The last time I saw Larry happy.

Your ultimate accountant

Your ultimate accountant:
You should have made him years back:
Someone should have told you that:

A man with muscles for cheeks,
Cheeks where his muscles should be:
New Zealand's Mussolini…

I'm just a lover in black
Bloodshot from a bout of you:
I have long since turned my back

Long since known just what to do:
Beyond all proposition
I've joined your Opposition.

Black cattle at dawn, Waiura

The fat black cattle
never seem to sleep

all night in the lower
paddock by the river,

like lover to lover
mooing to each other.

It's not as if they
do much else by day,

just watch one another
watching each other,

eyes wide brown and deep
don't earn a wink of sleep.

Part of the dark,
one-ton chunks of it,

the fat black cattle
awkward and bored

when first light spreads out
like the river in flood.

Call it the dawn, the Lord,
the Promised Land; whatever

what just a moment back
was a black black lake,

is now the lower paddock
in a full flood of light.

No transformation from Heaven
no light burst for them –

silhouettes left over
from the night before,

this moment of the Lord –
they are the one thing ignored.

Christina

I dream these nights of webs
and black spiders swinging:

my last circus I saw a man
swing the width of the Big Top:

everyone clapped: he bowed he
wore white supports on his wrists.

The lions and the tigers: one
jumped through a high hoop of flame:

I thought of you; mistook
their clapping for rain on the roof:

silence: then on came
a dark dancing Russian:

she climbed the rope to the very
top of the tent. She danced

turning over: they found a bird,
so rare they thought it extinct,

dead in the madhouse rafters;
black spiders swinging. She bowed,

everyone clapped. I came back
home, dreamed dreams of you who

I had imagined dead; everyone
clapping for more. They couldn't have enough!

Tonight is a web, Christina, black
spiders spinning; rain on the roof.

You house the moon

You have moved in upstairs.
I don't know what you do.
Except at night I know you
Sit up late. You watch the stars.

About all I know of you.
Merciless as migraine
You pace out my brain.
Maybe you want my view!

Headaches all the more.
I have this dream a load
Of timber's dumped on the road
Right outside my door.

One by one, just your way,
You drag each plank upstairs.
I see nothing for tears.
You hammer away

You house the moon. You join the stars.
You have come to stay.

Maintrunk country road song

Driving south and travelling
not much over fifty,
I hit a possum… 'Little
man,' I muttered chopping
down to second gear,
'I never meant you any harm.'

My friend with me, he himself
a man who loves such nights,
bright headlight nights, said
'Possums? just a bloody pest,
they're better dead!'
He's right of course.

So settling back, foot down hard,
Ohakune, Tangiwai –
as often blinded by
the single headlight of
a passing goods train as by
any passing car –

*Let the Midnight Special shine
its ever-loving light on me:*
they run a prison farm
somewhere round these parts;
men always on the run.
These men know such searchlight nights:

those wide shining
eyes of that young possum
full-beam back on mine,
watching me run over him…
'Little man,
I never meant you any harm.'

Every time it rains like this

Every time it rains like this:
rain from early morning falling
thick with light: the whole
wide world of our bay
has given in: rain: and nothing any
friend or fisherman can do

Every time it rains like this:
oilskins sweat in boatsheds:
well indoors: all's gone on for
far too long... I am
one with rain, no longer to
that woman there; we're through

Every time it rains like this:
I walk hangover beaches, make
no more sense of it:
in love with a winter woman,
a woman when she steams, I kiss
wet winter lips, return to you

Every time it rains like this

Of Dan and the Peacock

Of all the constellations,
Pavo the Peacock
is visible tonight.
Pavo has the whole
night to himself.
He struts terribly.

In our tangle of
fishing boats and baches,
the only light
is Digger Dan's.
He mends his net.
His lamp burns late.

Tomorrow night Dan
sails beyond Mana,
the whole of
Cook Strait to himself.
He will drag the dark;
bring home a peacock.

DRUNKARD'S GARDEN
1978

Drunkard's garden
(in tribute, Darkie)

Like Old Man Adam did.
Or Darkie when he died.
Like any man who moves
to other parts, we leave
our gardens after us.

Others move in to them.
They tend them; call them home.
I've left behind a share
of gardens. Like lovers.
And I move into yours.

This overgrown acre,
full of empties, Darkie!
A headland, refuge for
the heron, swan and wild
duck and drunkard; lover, child.

Friend to many
(in memory, Rupert Taylor)

The river runs through jonquils
Flowers on all the window-sills:

We will join you when we die
We will wander these green hills:

Friend to many, man, goodbye.

Two Winter settings

1

I knew a girl who
came from where the blue
lupin flower grew, oh
such a girl I knew

where lupin flowers grow
as blue as her blue
eyes against the snow.
So, the girl I know.

2

Taiaroa Heads, I've never
seen them floating so, so
easy on the light as
land can float on sea.

Low cloud slides south;
the albatross lift off;
warm breezes blow. Far as
eye can see, and further, snow.

Ana gathering cones on Battle Hill

When I do not know of what
to sing or speak – what tune,
what word – I watch and wait
the slow rising of the moon:

the moon so slowly rising,
a man can only wait
and watch and maybe sing
songs, speak words, of love or hate.

The moon last night in storm.
I watched it rage above
Battle Hill until the dawn.
That song was one of love.

Up there today among those
pines, we could, you thought, have been
aboard some ship in wild seas,
creaking jib, rib and beam.

I know of the many moons,
the shadows and the phases.
I know of as many women,
sung them silver phrases:

a moon for the river,
another for the sea.
This moon, tangled as ever.
You, of these dark trees to me.

Girl with black eye in grocer's shop

No hiding it, a proper
bloody mess. Lucky she's still
a left eye left at all.
She smiles back as usual.

The man she lives with – plans to
marry soon as his divorce is through –
he beats her up often.
Never quite this bad though.

About as much as we know.
No idea why: suspects some
other man maybe. No
difference, result's the same.

We know her scene by heart,
black eye, the bruises. Apart
from that, not a bad looker,
the sort of mystic hooker.

She smiles again, shows she's brave;
buys groceries for two, still in love.

Words on a first waking

Recall those dreams – at 2 a.m.
you call them poems – that one of home,
your father, huge, alive; the rooms
of that old house, themselves like dreams:

you spoke of him, your dad, his forced
retirement. Clenched like a fist,
death by slow cancer. You went down
south to see him; found half the man.

Recall him now; recall that dream
you called a poem at 2 a.m. –
that world of house and father deep
down south. And so, you drift from sleep;

you dress. Deliberate; beautiful,
as if you had a wardrobe full –
the same tight jeans and shirt you threw on
yesterday. To think us strangers then:

all lovers like to think they're not!
It's your world, love. You wander out
alone into the living room,
alone into another dream.

Four songs

1 *Snow song*

'I miss you when it snows' –

But cynics say it snows
in that demented fellow's
country barely once a year –

I say (and pray you hear)

'it snows here every day.'

2 *Love song*

I will hide in these dark trees.
           No one will ever
           find me here. An
animal, no more a man,
           crouched on hands and knees.

           So strange, my lover
lit in that great house below.
           She glows so; knows so!

           I will call on her,
make love to her, tomorrow.
           The taut bellied moon
           so low now, low. Soon
the sun must rise; I must go.

3 *Boy's song*

Above our house there is a track.
It winds its way across the hills.
Hot afternoons the hills turn blue
And darker blue until they're black.

My father used to carry me
In a battered blue back-pack.
He used to take me high, high up
That winding high-hill track.

When I was old enough to walk,
We walked together, my dad and me.
When I got tired he gave me piggybacks.
I sometimes fell asleep like that.

Last week I watched my father walk
Away from me, up that same track.
The hills have turned from blue to black
So many times. Still he's not come back.

4 *Recitative: Cloudy Bay*

White gulls blow inland now, your
eyes a winter closed. To say
we miss you's true. That we do;
wintered these months in the bay;

looking. No, not for you. We
know you're dead. Even the young,
those who don't remember you,
know that. Like they know your song:

they sing it every time they
see seagulls blown inland from
this winter shore. And true, they
sing that the drowned may hear them.

Those eyes; such mist

Sea mists from the upper inlet
lift, the morning hills afloat.

I dream of the several men who've
sailed seven seas; their many mists;

wake again to your love
as thick dreams clear; a dream of masts,

a dream that no man ever
saw your eyes like this.

I have lost all voice. I kiss
those eyes, our voyaging; such mist.

No Exit
(for Michael Smither)

              box-thorn and bamboo
wind-breaks round the coastal farms:
narrow roads that only go
headlong for the sunset.

Bring tokens with you, charms;
a letter, stone or wind-chimes:
dreams from the world left behind
worlds behind the mountain...

Egmont dropping in the rear-
vision mirror as you drive
drunk with all love lost in mind.

You will know it somewhere near,
of this alone, quite certain:
a man can go no further.

Birth of a son

My father died nine months before
My first son, Tom, was born:
Those nine months when my woman bore
Our child in her womb, my dad
Kept me awake until the dawn.
He did not like it dead.

Those dreams of him, his crying
'Please let me out love, let me go!'
And then again, of his dying...

I am a man who lives each breath
Until the next: not much I know
Of life or death; life-after-death:

Except to say, that when this son
Was born into my arms, his weight
Was my old man's, a bloody ton:

A moment there – it could not stay –
I held them both. Then, worth the wait,
Content long last, my father moved away.

Wagoning, up Moonshine
(for Kristin)

He plucks cress; water runs muddy.
He bends to drink, his image blurs.
The stream runs clear. He drinks
Till short of breath, falls back asleep:

Dreams of hawks on the upper
Current of the Moonshine wind, of
This wind's low moan. His dream
Burns clear, of her; of making love,
Whisky from water so pure.

Assumption, 1975

Baptism by river water

We have come a long way,
some would say too far;
beyond what others think
we should have done. You blink.
That was yesterday.

Your old man rose and spoke
of horses and love,
then turned into a tree;
which left just you and me.
I lit up a smoke.

Again, quick as a wink
and change of a verse,
today is tomorrow
and that is long ago.
Have yourself a drink,

watch the river below
make love with the light.
Together in this land,
much we don't understand.
Call it tomorrow.

The ancient clydesdale stands
still as the morning.
The trees now all that move,
a sigh of pines; rough love;
our laying on of hands.

For Kristin and Tom on a stormy morning

Last night the moon took one
Hell of a hiding: and then
this morning on the headland,
a colony of pied stilt, so
delicate, so very
timid really, in the
face of such a storm:
in military formation, they
stood it out and no
one budged or threatened them –
strength in numbers or some
such joke, I don't know! –

What I do know though,
that when I clambered up home,
my lady and baby both
brought back to mind that
battered moon, those small
brave birds in storm: so
timid at the window,
delicate and warm.

The men of Moonshine
(in memory, Chris Glennie senior)

The men of Moonshine now
are not the men that were:
where Glennie fought the law
these play a weekend war.

*Chris Glennie died a score
of years ago and more.*

Another breed of man –
if breed of man he be –
has pitched his pre-built house
on hills for all to see.

One of such a lucky few –
an exclusive way of life –
he wouldn't swap his view;
would rather swap the wife.

*Chris Glennie lived a score
of this man's days and more.*

The mists beyond Rock Hinge –
the hills behind slam-to –
drink up, a one last binge,
last distiller of the dew!

The man in his new home
has ended up alone;
has ended having nightmares
he is not anymore.

*Chris Glennie's come to haunt him,
to even up the score.*

My father today

They buried him today
up Schnapper Rock Road,
my father in cold clay.

A heavy south wind towed
the drape of light away.
Friends, men met on the road,

stood round in that dumb way
men stand when lost for words.
There was nothing to say.

I heard the bitchy chords
of magpies in an old-man
pine… *My* old man, he's worlds

away – call it Heaven –
no man so elegantly
dressed. His last afternoon,

staring out to sea,
he nods off in his chair.
He wonders what the

yelling's all about up there.
They just about explode!
And now, these magpies here

up Schnapper Rock Road…
They buried him in clay.
He was a heavy load,

my dead father today.

Liz
(with your left hand crippled)

I know your dreams are dreams of
waking with the man you love:

whoever in those dreams that
good man be, you have his heart…

I dreamt last night of you, Liz,
you, and every man had eyes

for some bird else: we were at
some bar. You sat like a cat,

queen of your corner, sizing
each bird up, hypnotising

every feathered one. They slowed
together. Then in a cloud

they rose across the garden,
the moon herself now hidden…

Planets and a thousand stars
retreated. You flexed claws

slowly, your left claw crippling.
I woke appalled, applauding.

Up Battle Hill

Trees move because the wind
moves them. They rock asleep.
The wind does not let up.
This moment has no end.

Light on the river moves
as if to move away.
Trees, wind, light, river, stay.
As you do too, far loves.

COLLECTED POEMS
1980

Rainbows, and a promise of snow
(for Alistair Campbell)

1

Winter means one side or other of
the shortest day. Our birthdays both
are on that good side, friend, of
solstice. Winter is a warm hearth;

rainbows, and a promise of snow.
Or so life's been for me this last
half-life of sixteen years. Days go
so very slow they say, so fast.

It matters not. A good mate dies,
another goes abroad or mad.
It matters neither way. What does,
what always will, is that we load

the fire high with logs. She's a
winter this! bull-seals barking in the bay.
If she don't snow soon, I tell you
friend, she's never going to.

2

Sixteen and just left school
I dumped my books and hiked
four hundred miles south;
hitched-up where I liked:

barbaric coast, barbaric winds
madder than I knew could blow:
what better making of friends,
a promise of snow.

I go to the river, friend,
walk along with the flow;
far as third bend,
far as I go:

remembering time goes
so very fast, so slow:
solstice and birthdays,
a promise of snow.

A mad wind has risen,
the bull-seals bark at the moon:
I have a knee-high son;
you, a grandchild soon.

My chance to wish you cheers,
we've many good miles to go.
Here's rainbows (whisky tears),
a promise of snow.

Hilary
(for Hone Tuwhare)

I too had a lean
aunt. She died at thirty.
Like yours, from Tb.
She was a cross between
mother and sister
but better than either.
She left five kids, and me.
I was aged ten
in the middle of winter.

A northern cousin
found a bird dying that morning.
He brought it to his mother, Joan,
one of Hilary's three sisters.
Joan froze. Then burst into tears.
She knew it was Hilary,
the youngest and most frail,

the one who wrote poems,
the one they called
'the Little Poet of Pangatotara',
the one who never got over
the flood of '55,
the year the Motueka River
rose and covered the farm.

There was silt through everything.
There was silt through Hilary's lungs.
She had strange dreams
the whole of that last year.

One, about me –
I have her letter still
telling of how
I'd one day walk out on stage.
Who would have believed it!

Hilary did.
And not long after, died.

I went by the farm today
but didn't go in.
Her husband lives there still,
a prosperous farmer
who dabbles in the arts,
happily remarried.

I could only watch
the river flow past the farm,
the Tasman mountains heave through mist,
the poplars hold the light apart.
And I thought for
a moment I saw
Hilary wave from the farmhouse door.

The rain quickened.
Soon everything –
the riverflat farm,
the mountains, river and poplars –
was blurred.

It was
years since I'd cried.

Four Manly verses

1

So much bare flesh, so very
smooth, brown as any berry,
utterly untouchable,
a man can only babble,
dream the unattainable,
stutter the impossible.

2

The loneliness of summer,
the over-forty runner:
SWIM BETWEEN FLAGS!
RESCUE PHONE ONE-ONE-ONE:
once a man has blown
youth, oh, once the bird has flown,
man drowns alone, blood and bone.

3

The fat and middle-aged all
out in force, out for a ball:
all end up in the kitsch
lounge bar perving at the beach:
sun, salt; the seven-year itch,
the gold flesh out of reach.

4

Meantime, lover by lover,
the young in the sun, never
heard of cancer of the skin;
horizoned there, the dorsal fin;
ever asked the price of sin,
Sonya, Barry, Brian, Lyn.

Salt man
(for Frank Sargeson)

Some man called you once
Salt Man. I would not,
could not, better that.
Nothing's won by chance –
I know that now –
it's where you strike
that matters most. Like
nothing's ever new.

This, to do with you?
For sure it is, Salt
Man, your great heart's vault;
with all things true –
back-roads of the heart;
pub; the bull's-eye dart.

Sailor's morning

Red sky at night
Shepherd's delight
Red sky at morning
Shepherd's warning

Storm light, red as the old shepherd's warning.
We always as children said 'Sailor' instead.
And always as children we were safe beside
A calm summer sea, blue in the morning.

I came down today like an outlaw to town.
The small local school was ringing its bell
Calling the kids from home, hot porridge, all
Those mornings ago I've nearly forgotten.

I make the gates, 9 a.m. I'm dead on time.
A newly-installed schoolmaster-cum-minister
Eyes me as if I were child-molester,
Satan-returned. I'm just trying to get back home!

Imagine addressing the locals…
'Ladies and Gentlemen of my home town,
I returned this morning saddle-sore down
The valleys till I came to those skyline hills'

(I point out the window of the hall)
'Like every poor bastard born these parts
I cleared out soon as I could' (applause; paper darts)
'Now, Ladies, Gentlemen, I return to Hell:

I must inform you though, there's a price on my head' …
It is here I always come-to, shouting that warning.
And the light wakes me up, turning red,
Storm light, red as the old shepherd's morning.

We always as children said 'Sailor' instead.

Return to Drunken Bay

I thought once if I one day
ever gave the booze away,

images would come my way
I never knew existed.

Instead I feel half-past-dead.
Friends they call me half-mast Fred.

Nineteen days and dry nights now
see me beached, a stranded scow

where white gulls nest, squawk and row:
nineteen nights and days now dry,

level-headed asking, why
stave off death, why even try?

I lie dead; like it somehow.
Gulls have taken over now.

All you have is this beached scow.
Listen, if you dare, for screams –

even the dead have their dreams.
Listen too for creaking beams.

Check for dry-rot; check each scar.
I let it all go far too far:

but like it, the way things are –
white waves near; one cold white star.

Return to Rangitoto

His days were full of maps
of places visited:
his nights as full of dreams
of friends long dead.

He had one tattered map,
island of black granite;
and one recurring dream
as sure as night.

All day on whisky he
would fight the demon drunk,
the nightmare-man who shared
his coffin bunk.

Two visions would not fade:
that map; that dream of her.
Most men pronounced him mad.
He did not hear.

He burnt that map – he had
directions well by heart –
he hit the road until
the road ran out.

The island was afloat,
volcanic on the light.
He was, men said, adrift.
I say, bereft.

Song for Tom

My son has come so far
to ask me something: what
I do not rightly know –
how far away a star?
how true, that stars burn hot?
how it is they glow?

I tell him, child, look,
these questions that you ask
have answers no man knows –
man writes many a book
just like he wears a mask.
Yet still the night sky flows.

He turns and goes away
outside into the dark.
I join him, take his arm.
There's so much left to say...
Far, far off, farm dogs bark;
fall silent now. Dead calm.

West Coast woman

I thought I had arrived; that this –
the shaking of hands, kisses from
strange ladies, speeches from a mayor –
I took this as arrival;

accordingly unpacked my bag, took a
stroll around the town, took a
show in with a stranger, later
stoned, made love with her.

Was I to be blamed? I was,
and for that matter, am, the
sort of man that people
point out as a man who has,

despite himself and those
who spite him most, arrived.
I felt so utterly
sure, surrounded as I

was by trappings such as these
I took for real; was had:
but come to understand it now,
understand your absence, your

refusal to join such mad
back-stabbing crowds: come
now humbled, to the closed
door you open.

Death of the poet preacherman

His tendency to preach through his verses
Became in the end, the critics agree,
His end. Abandoned by his images
Of stars and apple trees in bloom, the sea,

Of mountains melting to the sea, he died.
His funeral was packed. The critics and preachers
Made speeches, cracked quips; a few even cried –
Their universities and churches

Closed for the day. The only place open –
And where he would have been himself had he
Not been waylaid, packed in a box to ripen –
The Peep-O-Day. They drank the house whisky,

Recounted anecdotes: and all of them
About his drinking bouts; none to do
With blackouts, starless nights, spring without bloom,
Hangover mornings forever without dew;

Those he loved and lost. Or how, when he lost,
Refusing sentiment, he took up, rather,
Role of preacherman-in-verse; sort of priest,
Confessor, drunkard; sort of, my father.

April Fool

*It's the old tricks is best tricks
cause only the best tricks survive*

So,
up behind our hill
behind the macrocarpa belt
this God-almighty glow.

A fire first I thought how will
the engine ever get up there?

I changed my mind I thought those
new neighbours they're
always having parties.
Not like at our place.

I clambered up, wanting most I guess
a rock-and-roll band whacking
shit from up the hill. Floodlights,
everything I thought the whole
damn lot.

Instead, full on and lifting
out of heavy cloud,
the moon. Up to her old
tricks I thought.

River woman songs
(for Kristin)

1

We have not made love
since I had to leave north

since our silver turned over
when the full moon was new.

We will make love tomorrow
every bend of the river.

2

I lie down with the lamb.
Survival is my game.

My dreams are of you,
of nights, days left behind;

dreams of slow daybreaks,
sun on iced paddocks.

3
A joyless journey north
a woman's twisted mouth;

she smiled at times when time
was running to her rhyme.

I knew I had to leave her,
join you by the river.

4
You wait first movements,
the kid inside you kicking.

I watch your eyes for hints,
each dawn, their flickering.

We walk by the river often;
a daughter or a son.

Requiem

They say 'the lighthouse keeper's world is round' –
The only lighthouse keeper that I know
Inhabits space, his feet well clear of ground.
I say he is of light, of midnight snow.

That other lighthouse keeper – he they say
Whose world is round – is held responsible
For manning his one light by night; by day,
For polishing his lenses, bulb and bell.

My man, my friend who lately leaves, is quite
Another type. He climbs no spiral stairs:
But go he does, for good, to man the night;
To reappear, among his polished stars.

RUNNING SCARED
1982

Running scared

Do these things matter – to shake
that shower now, dishes,
to make the solitary bed.
Far as anyone's concerned
a man could as well be dead.

And far as that bitch goes,
she'll be seeing the lawyer today –
bet her stale life on it, mate –
and it won't be just my blood
she's after, but settlement-date.

A good motel this,
no worry over the dog
and no questions asked –
drank whisky late into the night,
collapsed like an old ram cast.

The Kaikouras this morning,
snow-clad and dazed, blink
on ocean and coast, gaze
and seem to smile. A man can't help think
of happier days!

the honeymoon trip down the coast
and the moon dripping honey,
the young man and his wife,
hot honey on toast! 'And money
won't buy you happiness or life':

how dead fucking true, mate,
but I learned it too late.
Just hope the kids cope.
Cars slide by. Enough, the choices,
this man alone's: hope or the rope.

Enough! to count the cars
sliding by, remember the bars
where the women and jokes were shared.
Scars smart now like the stars through tears –
a man and his dog, running scared.

After separation

The images of young kids,
abandoned toys left strewn;
this drawing of three people
(Mummy-Daddy-me I guess you'd say
had I bothered to ask)
stuck knee-level on the wall.

*I only noticed it, Tom,
after you'd gone home.*

Or today, this morning first thing,
crashing round my kitchen full of
empties and butts, find floating in a
bottle full of fresh water –
a flower, a daisy of sorts,
brought in from the garden.

*Sorry, Tom,
I never noticed at the time.*

But read what I like into it –
your saying, 'Yes, this house of
Dad's is my house too
like Mummy's is uptown,
a picture and a flower to prove it.
So you better believe it.'

*Only wish you'd told me, Tom,
before you went home.*

Call this house your own while I'm
squatting in it – your second home –
and that is all I am,
a squatter of sorts, a refugee
who entertains his little boy
from foreign parts.

*And I'm learning your tongue, Tom,
I'm learning it fast.*

You know, after your last visit
and after you left,
I crept round this old joint like I'd
woken too early for Christmas.
Stumbled blind from room to room
fearful of what I might find.

Beyond the brink

He sees her cross the road,
the child with her. She won't
see him, she never did.
Voice chokes in his throat.

Her head is with the shrink,
heart cracked. He's seen her walk
away, beyond the brink
of letters, phone calls, talk.

Should he be tough?
At times he thinks he should be –
not turn a hair or give a stuff
or let on he knows she

sits up sleepless, crying;
stalks these city streets;
sees herself as dying
alone between cold sheets.

A mutual fate, he'd guess,
born losers both? She slows
her pace. But nonetheless –
it must be so – she goes.

Words for Tina
(barmaid, Southern Cross)

Child,
your wide eyes wild –
may they never be stilled
by father, brother, lover,
tonight or
any other…

You move among
a gaggle of girls –
something like the wild
pony I loved as a child:
there was no such thing
as 'breaking her in'.

She came to me one day –
I was feeding out hay –
she bowed into my hands
shyly, as if to be scolded:
as she lowered her eyes
I noticed they smouldered.

But it's back to the bar,
there are drinks to be poured.
The men, they're out to impress;
their women, painted and bored.
You move among them,
a shy pony in a dream…

So, woman –
keep your wild eyes wide;
every man you serve
thinking himself adored.
Christina, Christ in a
word, you have no Lord.

Brother Lynch

Old Boys – the boys you knew in shorts and
socks, the boys like me – they come to
visit regularly.

Just as I did yesterday, brought
two bottles from
my motel fridge, imagining that three
or a half-dozen would seem
I'd come – not to talk
and talk to you alone, old Lynch –
but come simply
to hit the piss.

I'd never seen you out of uniform,
a chalky black soutane,
a white coat in the science lab.

You wore a green shirt yesterday,
a man at home.
Your old eyes shone.

Of course your Old Boys call
with conversation pieces like
'Do you remember Grant Malloy?'
or 'What of Kevin Mahon?'

– What else (your words), 'in every
man there is the boy,
in every boy the man.'

No, in green shirt yesterday
and me a travel-weary happy man,
we spoke of other things, of
the marriages void of love,
the evening sunlight in the trees,
the winter seamists rolling in.

This was so unlike the school
a thousand miles north you
taught me in – 'They
move us oldies on!'

No seamists there – no sea –
and I never hung round
past four o'clock to watch
the evening in a tree.

But do so now –

and see myself, kept in late,
detention yet again,
heading for the schoolgate –
the boy inside the man,
a thousand poems to write –

the amputated plane trees,
the empty tennis courts,
the grassy bank above where
we smoked our cigarettes –

and in the distance, out of
uniform, the Brothers,
mowing lawns or walking,
solitary men, no
women waiting them.

I leave you, Brother Lynch,
bifocalled bright-eyed man;
can only wish that others
see you as I do –
nothing celibate or sorry,
nothing sad about you.

Meantime, warm cheers, cold beers,
good Brother Lynch,
you have your Heaven yet –
green shirt open to the neck –
an old man
blinking at the sunset.

Passing through

1

Two towns you only pass through,
don't even notice probably,
for that man there means life. His
wife, for one example, comes
originally from here. He, he comes from there.
How they ever came to meet,
fucked if I know. Or
fucked if I care.

2 *Near Manaia*

A white horse beside a white church.
A white church beside a white horse.
I'm not sure which I prefer,
but, please
                keep things
just as they are.

Returned Serviceman

The drinking-driving blitz is on,
    We take the back roads home.
Another old soldier gone,
    A man who fought the Somme.

We won't meet at the cenotaph
    Recalling wars he fought –
No obituary or photograph
    At the Magistrate's Court.

At closing-time Len left the pub –
    What better time to leave –
Yelled out 'I'll catch you down the club'
    To Jerry, me and Steve.

Too far gone to wink or think,
    Lenses fogged as a sauna,
His left-hand headlight on the blink,
    A cop around the corner.

Len's old Morrie wasn't worth much
    And Len a dead duck –
'Anyway, she was short on clutch
    And me, I'm short on luck!'

Len looked befuddled beside his heap,
    Crumpled as a fallen flag.
'Please take a big breath, long and deep
    And blow into this bag.'

The Court was like the Dawn Parade.
    The cop gave evidence
Like he'd led the Light Brigade.
    And not a twitch or wince

From Len, V.C., D.S.O.
    Medals polished up;
The same three-piece those years ago
    He wore when signing up.

Five hundred dollars, licence scrapped,
    A hotel drinking ban:
Len laughed it off, but something snapped,
    He was broken, man.

And fading fast, before his time –
    Unbroken by a war –
He lives in town now, drinks cheap wine,
    Wonders what he fought for.

Ancient taupata, Bottle Creek
(for Tom 2½)

1

This wizened tree has had
more than, say, a hundred
children through her limbs;

in her gnarled way
has taught them to climb.

You see them any day
climbing under, through her,
into, over her.

But what you do not hear
when night-time finally comes –

when what was light is dark
and what was once a branch
is now a nightmare catacomb –
soft sighs. She whispers them,
'Go now, lovers, children, home!'

2

I watched this morning Tom
alone for his first time
approach that tree and climb
from limb to wizened limb.

She bowed, like pretending
he, and only he,
had ever climbed that tree.
For him alone, such bending!

So he climbed to the very
top, so slowly; very
carefully picked and brought me down
the highest poison-red berry.

Death in the street
(for Tom, 4½)

A widow of four days –
and it's rained
every day since –

she walks up the road
her red umbrella high.
You ask if she cried:

*Do old people cry
when their cats or dogs or
dads die?*

and *where* and *how* and *why?*

A widow of four days –
she seems already used
to walking alone –

only last week
she and her husband
walked past up the street,

stopped by to speak.
She chatted
about an old friend newly dead.

He looked impatient; shuffled his feet.

Was he drowned? Your questions
roll on as ever:
or was he run over?

and I, as ever,
explaining.
And why, you ask, *the umbrella?*

it's already stopped raining.

Bottle to Battle to Death

From Bottle to Battle to Death,
places where we lived from
meeting up one crazy night to
splitting up – a child in tow –
a nightmare of an afternoon.

Bottle Creek was our first home,
a boathouse perched on stilts.
The heron thought us one of them.
We paced the mudflats; full tide, swam:
no place (they said) to bring a baby up in.

To Battle Hill where once, one
hundred years before you or I were born,
a poet of a chief held back the Poms.
He let the land fight for him.
Our child was born here, Tom.

Those days, some days, were good,
the nappies flapping at the clouds,
the clouds crash-landing on the hills.
And white as mushrooms on the slopes,
the sheep; at lambing-time, the hawk.

We gave our child Kahu for
a second name, in honour of that hawk.
Our silences invaded us –
the dark hills, sky, the hovering.
It was, for us, an end of talk.

The move then down the valley,
back beside the estuary, the ancient
homestead, Death (and not D' Ath).
We didn't stand a chance.
We stalked each other, minute by minute.

I would watch the shy pukeko. They
would run out on the road, crazy as
the clouds that charged the hills.
The cars would always win the game.
Pukeko dead, a dull blue flame.

And then, of course, there was you.
And to say I loved you was true.
And that I hated you was true.
I thought though, if we lie down,
lie down low, we may come through.

Instead, minute by minute, we stalked
each other out. Sometimes we walked
the hills together, Tom in the back-pack,
the dog forever chasing sticks.
And then an afternoon, quite casually, I talked

of 'going our own ways'. I can't
remember now what brought me to it.
Maybe you said, we can't go on this way.
Or, maybe best we call it all a day.
I don't know now. But you went away.

Dead bird

1

I have not slept – or if so,
woken from nightmares full of
fountainheads of blood, of
headless dogs, of bloodied snow –

not slept since the last full moon,
returning from travelling to
shoreline shack last Saturday,
a dead bird in my room.

And many friends, some past, some
I see each day, have made their
brief appearances. So there
should be no surprise you come –

or rather, stand, dead still – in
one such dream: big dogs pumping
blood; the snow, etc. Except,
you stand so small, so alone.

I write, to ease the flood of
longing, fears for you, dead bird.
And I would I could send flowers
scarlet as your midnight blood.

2

Things happen slowly, their
lives don't change. Your death left
few stunned. The night you died
they got stoned –

could as easily flown to Sydney
or taken the ferry to Picton
or next day punched a man –
and not even your lover

or even your driver… So,
at a show last night I told
a poem for you; and everyone
cried like they knew you.

And travelling today through
the flat sad provinces of home,
no more backbones
worth breaking,

no journeys… Better to die
than fucked up on crutches, you say?
provincial parish churches
pointing at a bored sky.

3
We drove the backstreets of some
surreal town. Your boyfriend was
dead – or if not dead about
to die. What was worse

was that neither cared. I asked
a traffic cop the way. He
burst into tears, into song.
He then burst into blossom.

You said 'Let me take the wheel'
and off we sped down Highway
Number One. 'How does it feel?'
I asked. But I'd meant to say

something quite different – like, 'What
age would your child be today
were he alive?' or, 'Should we wait
your boyfriend's funeral?'

I came to later. At that
moment you came too. We balled
all night, no smalltalk, no chat,
no chance to ask why you called.

New words

New words, the words I have not
told, they gather for the night.

I send them out each day, each
tolling on its own. They reach

I know not where. They bounce back
reeling, some ready to break,

some merely echoing. They
bring back their news of the day

told in each one's way. They come
back tired, relieved to be home.

These words, the words I have not
told, they settle for the night.

Then, and only then, I light
the lamp, work on them, work late;

coax and grill. Interrogation
does not let up till the dawn.

Some nights, a few surrender,
tell me all I need know – her

dreams, the rhythms of her heart.
That's when there's a poem in it.

APPROACHES TO PAREMATA
1985

October in the bay

1

Their mating is taking place
blatantly in front of us,
two tall blue white-faced herons –

they can teach us a thing or
two or three on four-day play!
For four days now around our

bay of bright painted shacks,
a couple of herons
have pecked and played and shied and

out of nowhere flown past in
unison, in pendulous flight –
four days we have borne the sight

of what – when it does happen,
when the event does take place –
will last hardly a moment.

And you can be damn sure
that we who have watched hardest
will miss it – like it flashed past us –

leaving us, the academic
bird-watchers we are at best,
the peck and play, shy and fight,

inhabiting a shoreline where we
can dream only, only dream
of such slow pendulous flight.

2

Old Mr Mitchell
whose wife Mrs Mitchell
died a month or so ago

is burning grass cuttings on the beach.
I watch him through
a pair of binoculars.

Through one end
he looks close up, friendly
almost. Through

the other end not so
friendly. Indeed, ferociously
far-away.

Which is probably the way
God and Mrs Mitchell
are watching him today:

Games Time in Heaven:
Looking Back on Loss –
to move you must throw a seven.

The fire's billowing
blue smoke across the bay.
Mr Mitchell's fire's underway.

My eyes water.
God and Mrs Mitchell, too,
are maybe shedding just a tear or two.

Patea 1983

1

They have only time to spend
(and an odd 20-cent piece
on a space-invader game) –
the people of Patea.

The local meatworks closed down.
A farmer tells you, 'Silly
bastards brought it on themselves,
they've no one else to blame.'

'How sure are you of that?'
you ask him now. But he has
cows to milk, business in hand –
'Someone has to work the land!'

2

So this is it, Patea,
the town
closed down. Only the river
moves – and that, hardly at all.

They say negotiators
are coming to town next week.
An overseas crowd wants to
buy it 'lock, stock and barrel'.

That's what they reckon down the
pub. And the woman at the
dairy said that's what *she* heard.
'Where there's smoke there's fire,' she said.

3
Fringes of the King Country,
fringes of Taranaki,
time-tattered and forgotten.
The river is always brown.

A half-caste kid in denim
chats you up for a dollar;
changes it into 20s.
He does not notice you leave.

And nor does anyone. You
cruise through town like the river;
sluggishly slope off. You do.
You have a job to go to.

Arthur Allan Thomas

We don't go much on saints and
Thomas ain't no saint.

But driving today slowly
through his fogged swamped lowland –

Mercer, Pukekawa,
a pub and burger bar most towns –

I spotted Thomas and a mate
drinking in the corner of a lounge bar.

The river ran close by.
A dredge was working the bar.

The jukebox sang of
Far-Away Eyes.

Which is all I've thought of since,
of Thomas's eyes, their lowland look,

fucked and far-away …
I know we're not hooked

on saints – as if that matters –
but we sure aren't short on martyrs.

Wedding party and after

Don't drink too much, Larry,
you've still got to put
the horse through her paces,
a man called Mike said yesterday.
And I, another wedding guest,
thought he spoke of Ros
(the bride I'd given away an
hour before). I've heard
women called dogs –
a horse, never!

But sitting today beside
a turquoise motel swimming pool a mile out of town,
remembering all the things the people
did and talked about last night –
one woman got so drunk she pulled
her husband's pants down yelling,
Look at this I've got
to fucking live with it! –
I got back to
thinking about you,

thinking, too,
of horses and paces
and all the things
people put each other through.
And later on the man
whose wife had pulled his pants down
threw up. And in between –
between that, and staring out the moon –
he yelled, I think to me,
It's all a fucking swindle, mate!

Six summer sestets

1

At any moment – makes no difference if
you're there to witness it or not –
windsurfers will be out on the inlet;
and in the shallows, especially at sunset,
a group of Islanders will be dragging a net.
The feeling of being there; but not part of it.

2

A couple of kids, not long out of school,
have brought fish and chips down to the beach to eat.
I watch them through the big binoculars.
They are immersed, totally, in eating.
And now they're either playing or fighting
and their fish-and-chip paper is flying.

3

When I run out of things to write about,
I'm asked what I do ... I pick up the big
binoculars I keep on hand –
either hanging from a six-inch nail or
somewhere on the jetty – I pick them up,
turn the music up; scour inlet, shoreline, sky.

4

I like people who travel on their own;
no threat about them.
One man, he drives his car along the beach
then reverses back up. I watch him
hours on end. He is a pest, for sure.
But there's something oddly likeable there.

5

Two girls, one plain, one pretty,
have wandered up the sand track.
The plain girl lives locally.
The other, fifteen, very
proud and pretty in purple bikini –
she won't be back.

6

The fairy tern outclasses the light –
but, I'm reminded now, depends on it;
reminded, once again: for shadow
an object needs light ... I can put it
differently: for light *you* need shadow.
Like the fairy tern. You both know that.

Lisa from Manjimup

We sleep behind flat sheets of tinted glass.
We slide them open in the morning
Look out across the turquoise pool
At tinted plate-glass sliders opening.

I've hidden out all day behind my tinted door
Listened to the inevitable
Team of girl netballers squealing round the pool.
They're from a small town, two hundred miles south.

One, a blonde called Lisa, asks me
Will I write a poem for her? I say Maybe.
And what's it going to be about?
I say I don't know, I haven't written it.

She reckons she can't wait. Nor, Lisa,
Can I. And this – for what it's worth – is it.

Wave song

I want to come back as a wave
that in summer breaks in on beaches
full of people and fibrolite baches;
stroke delicate down, slowly
slip off your tiny bikini.

I want to come back as a wave
that scatters among the bathers
go down as they come up for breathers
splatter and spume at their ankles
make every body beautiful.

I want to come back as a wave
so always near, so out of reach,
so when they run back up the beach
their glowing bodies fading home
my salt will still be upon them.

I want to come back as a wave
that in winter moves on.
No one will know where I'm gone.
I will cruise some desolate part
say Shag or Puysegur Point.

I want to come back as a wave,
regather forces, spend myself;
in the spring, move in on estuaries
attend to the mating of stingrays –
tidal, lengthening days.

I want to come back as a wave.
And though I love the estuaries,
bare coasts, autumn memories –
I want to lift you now and float you
as you, too, come as a wave.

SELECTED POEMS
1987

We are nearly neighbours

We are nearly neighbours.
But seldom see each other.
Which is the way it is,
the way things are.
We wouldn't have it different.

Between our shoreline houses
that face each other
over mudflat and shellbank and channel
and over on Jack's side
a rocky shore,
between our shoreline houses,
the tides and winds and silences.
We wouldn't have it different.

This morning, the tide right out,
I walked out over
mudflat and shellbank,
stood at the edge of the channel,
spoke to Jack across it.
There was no need to shout.
We wouldn't have it different.

Waikato river song

A South Waikato fog is hanging
low across:
the river out there somewhere
moving.

A friend of mine
traced her family,
the whakapapa of her tribe.
She said it was like the river,
this river,
Waikato,
its fogs, its bends.

She said she'd seen her river
lost in fog.
Like this morning.
But always knew it out there
somewhere, moving.

Glimpse

My mother
out there on the other
side of the world, my brother
further out.

Where he was
none has been.
He sometimes talks of it,
likes to walk a lot;

spoke today of leaping
off and out again; then walked
away from me into the wind,
his great coat flapping.

Hitting 40

I like being this little bit older.
Given me more time to see the reason
every body has their season,
the shape of their cross on their shoulder.

I like being this little bit sadder.
Always thought it would last forever
and mostly funny if not clever,
the first to fall off the ladder.

Older, sadder — but wiser, never,
not on these heron legs, no:
that's when I say I got to go
hit the road. Which goes on forever.

ANGEL GEAR
1989

I wonder what the old man is thinking?

I have a dog, seventeen,
        Minstrel's the name.
He's led me across river and dream,
        taught me the game.

And a kitten, Patrick,
        an acrobat.
She belts out a trick.
        What does the old man think?

I never thought to ask him.
        And when I did
it was either too late or I'd
        forgotten the question.

Kitten purrs; Minstrel snores;
        clouds burst, rain pours.
Tomorrow morning check the tanks
        is what the old man thinks.

Foreign hotel

You have other heroes, don't
you now, proclaiming a Yeats
is in your midst. I wish he
were. For me, I'm booked into
a foreign hotel where the
steam rises as a man is
singing from far off, that death
is not in fact the end. I
thank heartily, hope for your
sake as much as anyone's
the gentleman is right. He
usually is. As the steam is
rising all over the place.
I wandered out late last night,
watched a wild cat cross
the lit door of a meeting house.
I may not be writing much
the letters you say you wait.
And for sure, I am no Yeats
and Yeats was just another
man singing from far off, a
cranky gentleman in a
foreign hotel, not even
sure about that question of
death; or those others of love;
but surely as this thermal
steam rises, know he was right.

Making tracks

The fishing boats are all out,
dinghies on moorings.
The long-liners will be back later.
The trawlers won't be in
till all bins are full,
it could be days.

And you ask, how long does it take
a track
to be a path! Like –

the first time the grassland is explored
the track left is
the track of one man,

the gentle tread of a lightfoot, say.

Another person comes another
day to the edge of the grassland.
Or down to the bay a morning
like this, the fishing boats out,
dinghies on moorings.

When ever they come, they stand,
they see the track of the first man
(the dinghy keel down the wet sand)
and if there's no better option,
follow it. (It's a track by then.)

It has something to do
with the long-liner, *Silver Spray*,
we watched this morning
motor out from the bay
for the groper reefs of Cook Strait.

The old man aboard is ninety,
fished with his father from French Pass,
went to sea when he was twelve.
They go back, father to father,
fishermen. There's a rock
named after one of them.

Some say it's him.

And if that's not a track,
the naming, in honour, of a rock,
I don't know what is!
No worry though, the
sea is calm, there's
no one on the grassland.
We are the first ones here, that's
right, the first ones born. So let's
start making tracks.

Spider song

I nudge the victim to his last
pulse, his last breath, last
flicker. I nudge him many
times more, sometimes all night and
the next day too. Until the
sun has long gone west and the
light in his eyes is utterly
out. When there is nothing left, like
love, I leave.

The man on the sandtrack said

'Looks like it's the end
of Jack Winter's dream.'

I never am to know if he
meant me or the weather:

but this evening south
the sky's in black leather –

in keeping with the time,
coming on strong.

I guess the same could be
said of me, grim

slant to mouth, wince
of pain or of mirth.

I never am to know what Jack Winter's
dream was, but the weather's

strutting its wares. And
it looks like the end.

Tora wind song

Blatant as the weather –
you either have me dancing or
you blow me right over –
the times we have together.

There is no easy measure –
the dance we dance is crazy:
I study you so closely
I am reading you for sure.

Other times you start to roll –
eyeballs first and then your head –
roll away on me and hide.
Those times there's nothing real.

Just now and then there's meaning –
like when the nor'westers drop.
Before a southerly sets up.
Just now and then, like this morning.

What dandelions think

It's still only early,
just three o'clock a hot
December day
and the dandelions
already asleep, you say.

Not surprising, I suggest.
If you'd been throwing
a yellow out like that
since early this morning
you'd need an early night.

Because that's what
dandelions do: think yellow. Yellow.
Nothing else. Lose it,
they run the risk of turning
blue, say; God help me, pink.

Yellow is what dandelions think.

Yellow

It is the yellow of
(guessed it) the
dandelion:

bees have
died for it, mis-
taking the sun.

That's how one
such story goes.
Yellow as that.

Probably
true, the story.
Any

story about
dandelions and yellow
has got to be.

For you,
remember it. Be
ready to die for it.

Yellow as that.

Bone flute

I blast bone flute for every bit of me,
spend out across the lake.
It won't be just Hinemoa hears me;
but she's the one has to.

Her people back as far as Big Canoe
will want to know the man that blew the flute.
Tutanekai. I make it
work like it's never had to.

It won't be just Hinemoa either
getting ideas about swimming the lake.
But she's the one I want and what
will happen, has to.

September 1st

1

Herons pace the shore as
herons do; a black
flotilla of shags is
rounding up fish;
I walk alone because I've
not got you.

But a man has to live.
I'm doing the
best I can. But nothing worth
say, dying for
is easy to live with;
I know that.

So hit me with your heaviest
ham of a fist,
I can take just
about anything
today, September first,
first day of spring.

2

The old man thinking aloud
is what I want to listen
to right now. Let him have his
say, let his be the lesson.

Be ready for his reason,
a sly slow quarter rhyme,
that takes you beyond the far rim
where you are the only one left in the room.

You hang from the fifth wall
and you notice the old man
is talking and you begin to start to remember
today is the first day of spring.

Clearing the ashes out

A black skin glove on the floor,
fingers pointing in,

gumboots and shovel covered in clay
outside the boathouse door;

and clearing the ashes out
this morning from the stove,

a lump of melted metal
size of a human heart,

shape of a woman kneeling,
her lower body beautiful,

her upper half in flames,
lava lifting, smoke

solidified. Death
in three short names.

Oterei rivermouth

I get to think that God
is somewhere there between the rivermouth and sea
glistening

helplessly
with only a broad sky a bored dog and me
listening.

Catching the tide
(in memory, John Clark, lost at sea)

I didn't join the search party;
watched it gathering at the cruising club;
came to watch the fishing boats instead.

I better be careful you don't become our Lycidas,
you silly old bugger, John,
seems like you've done it this time –
you tried hard enough last year,
drove your yellow Triumph Stag
north up the railway line,
met the Northerner travelling south.
The car – I never did like Triumphs –
the inevitable write-off.
I forget what happened after that
except that you walked away laughing
pissed beyond caring.

    STRICTLY NO FISHING WHILE ON THIS BRIDGE
the NZR sign reads.
Or is it
    STRICTLY NO WRITING POEMS WHILE ON THIS BRIDGE
        GAZING AT THE FISHING BOATS
        GRAZING HEAVY MOORINGS
           STRICTLY
      NO DREAMING OF OPEN SEAS

Cook Strait is deeper than coffin or urn.

I didn't join the party.
Join yours instead,
the Big One that never ends;
come to catch the tide, Clarkie,
turning as the fishing boats turn.

Not in this weather

The hand is not a fist
until that hand is clenched.

Like this frostbitten fist of winter
clenched at the windscreen.

There is no driving back.
And if there were

I couldn't; and wouldn't.
Not in this weather.

Rangitaiki road song

He died of a heart attack.
Some said it was sudden, knife in the
back.
I'm not so sure —
like, when it did happen
I was suddenly surprised
it hadn't happened before.

Those last few months
we saw him a whole lot more.
Friends reckoned — after the event! —
he was just trying to tell us.
They reckon that's obvious.
Again, I'm not so sure.

Or wasn't until today
walking by the Rangitaiki river
wrecked in my own roaring forties,
a winter sun steel enough
to make a man shiver;

thinking of the man we knew that **died**,
the man that nobody heard,
the shit of a life he'd had;
his last, sad, solitary hit —
the whole way out on it.
I prayed today beside the Rangitaiki;

got whacked this afternoon —
a fist of local head a lady
gave me yesterday;
later on with Poss
hit the Rangitaiki pub,
forgot for a while profit and loss.

The stars tonight are out,
they shaft and shiver
in league with the river.
Goodnight, I am all heart.
I have been since that winter sunlight
glanced me where it hurt. Goodnight.

Four plateau songs
(for Tom, turning 11)

1

I climbed the mountain to learn
I had no need to be there,
took a room further down;
could not have gone further.

I spend the most, most days now
inside of a hotel room –
a distant dad, a dizzy man,
on the edge of a mountain.

2

The lady at the pool table
has on a see-through dress.
Which is, I guess,
worth mentioning.

I mean, if she didn't
and I couldn't (see through it)
I wouldn't have thought
to mention it worth it.

3
A man asked me
last night in the house bar
just how it was
I could remember the poems.

I told him I could not forget them,
they're flesh and blood.
And your best poem? he asked.
I told him Tom.

4
Your mother loved this plateau
country, Ruapehu.
Our best times were here
of three years together.

We never got to climb
or ski or tramp or do
what people do on mountains.
But she comes with the view.

Sara

Your body has no flaw.
That must be a lie!
Maud Gonne had sad hands,
Angela's temper never opened doors.

Your body has no flaw.
I look for one daily,
the darkness of the valley,
the climb to your jaw.

Your body has no flaw.
I part the earth and sky
I witness birth
I pray at a bleeding door.

Your body has no flaw.
The black shag neither.
Nor the blue heron at prayer.
You live outside the law.

Your body has no flaw,
buttocks breast and thigh,
curved ankles where I lie;
your calves, another shore.

Your body has no flaw.

MAKING TRACKS
1991

Coming to it

Three kids down at the front gate
wait the school bus;
fog hung low down the valley,
the house in sore need of paint,
the bright washing on the line,
a Van Morrison morning.

A man without a dog is not a man.
You don't have to believe it,
you really don't.
But it's all to do with the farm gate,
the three kids waiting the bus,
the man singing, the man we're listening to.
He knows where buses go
and why they never painted the house;
and if it's songs about fog you want,
Van Morrison's your boy.

So come over here,
take a look:
the fog is lifting – or is it just drifting? –
the bus has taken the kids to school.
And there's a man singing.
Wait for it –
the bright-washing-on-the-line bit –
we're all just
coming to it.

Seven years

She gazes through the window.
Peers for all she's worth,
more than anyone is worth,
into a fogged mirror.

She's breathing, that's for sure.
What she's looking for
won't be looked at here,
not anywhere.

If I did rightly know
I'd tell her straight –
it does not exist,
not in mirror or window.

She must know that.
I mean, she's been told
and she's not out to be fooled.
She clenches fist,

smashes to shit
window, mirror.
Seven years, she insists,
is worth it.

It's rain today in Sydney

I never would have
dreamt it, that words –
the telling them –
could lead to this
this charmed crazed day.

I would have told it
differently, that last
bit anyway. But
that's where you come in,
spirit and lady,

and the rain
comes down. I never knew
rain could fall so.
As, too,
I hardly know your name

but know it has to do
with rain, with rain
and telling the story
telling it true
charming it crazy.

Place matters too –
to tell where we are:
miles high and one with rain
above two city streets,
Goulburn and Elizabeth.

After words

At least I care enough
to look you in the eye.
      At least I care
      enough to lie.

I've seen a lot of hurt,
the shattered shell of egos.
      If love survives,
        well then here goes!

In the name of honesty
we can break each other.
      In the name of love
      why bother?

e.g. I ended up
in some strange lady's bed.
      So what! such news
      may swell my head

and meantime shatter you
and shatter what we clutch,
      this fragile shell.
      Our love is such.

The same rule goes for me.
Just tell me like it's true
      I don't care what –
      I'll believe you.

That feeling-of-being-in-the-country

When you stop at some small country town
and some local –
after you've complimented them on their town –
says We like it it's a good community

you think of that group of people
for whom this place is town,
Reporoa, say,

everyone creating their own sort of light
throwing it out their kind of way
and you think of that community
and the communion of saints.

I never felt less
like wearing dark glasses
than in Reporoa this morning.

War history

We fought last night,
sheets and blankets and pillows
askew. Then slept.
My nightmares were mild
compared to such wild
Hell – woke
sweating in some far
corner of a foreign field,
trenches of night between us.
I crawled belly down
toward where I thought
I saw you last,
removed a pillow carefully
for fear it would explode;
felt you out long last
curled up in a dug-out of blankets;
reached for your hand –

crawled in from no man's land.

Rangitikei river song
(in memory, Rob Newcombe)

A man can only
find himself when lost.
Such country, this,
where all men are lonely:
plateau, hawk and rivermist:

country where a man at last
might lose himself, an end of talk;
find that gaunt-faced other
man who stalks these ridges:
plateau, rivermist and hawk:

no longer keeping eye
for crumbling edges,
lovers or the weather.
Listening, rather, to the river:
hawk and high plateau,
rivermist below.

DOWN THE BACKBONE
1995

A *new plateau song*

I have a son I love
as a father loves a son,
a woman I love
as a man loves a woman –

such love is huge
in its normality:
no one makes any
mention of the mountain

adrift above their town.
They know it's there
and don't need any
word of it from me.

I have a son I love
and there is fog on the
shoulder of the mountain
as a father loves a son.

The woman, same, she
comes from under the mountain.
I tell of my love for her
and the fog giving over.

A woman, boy and a man
walk down from the mountain –
such normality
needs no word from me –

except to say
the woman is the woman I love,
the boy, my son. I am the man.
And this is our mountain.

Why a man

a woman and child
stand on a beach
throw stones out to sea?

It's a flint stoned beach –
they are well armed –
this could go on for weeks.

The enemy? must be
the sea
and all the sea

does to a man
a woman and a child –
to do with horizons.

No wonder they throw stones.

Fire, as always

Where there's
smoke there's
fire were his
words. What her
words were

nobody heard

nobody was
sober or straight
and as always
the dead were wise
after the event.

Nobody heard

a solitary word
the woman spoke.
But there was
smoke, sweet smoke among us.
And fire, as always.

Old flames

The cabbage tree was, they said,
dead. There was nothing they
or anyone could do
now or any day –
how sorry they
were, and sad.

But the cabbage tree heard them –
they never noticed
it shaking its head:
it shook it so hard
stars were said to have spread
from where the cabbage tree stood:

a blossoming, new constellation
across that night sky south.
Someone said just
yesterday,
some fires
you can't put out.

Hey, Minstrel

I know you're there.
I can hear you listening.

        Parked, say,
between a highway and river –
the roadbuilders left space
for dogs, and people like us.
The odd driver toots, spots
a man without a dog.
That's okay, you had to
die when you did.
We chose the day.
The day chose us.
It wasn't till after we buried you
there was any fuss.
Then it was Christmas.
I called up an old mate and
gave up the piss.

I know you're there.
You came by last night
just as I was talking to
a woman with the moon in her hair.

Nothing unusual in that. The moon's
been hanging around
an awful lot lately.
But you were there for sure.
She kept asking if I was all right
and kept repeating her name
as if I didn't know her.

Strange, the times since you died.
But while there's space
for dogs and people, a place
a man can park his car
between a highway, say,
and a river;

                        or, more simply,
touch the moon, that's okay too.

Working the Genesis week

A working week ahead of me
I grab an early night
so can kick off Monday early
creating the light.

Tuesdays aren't much.
Tuesdays seldom are.
My normal Tuesday
I part the waters.

Wednesday's a trippy affair:
vegetation early on, later
the bit I like best, often
go overboard on blossom.

Thursday is strictly moon,
sun, planets, stars.
I like to place them, space them,
according to mood.

Friday's paraphernalia,
provide fish and fowl, food
for table and altar.
Friday night I like to get out;

sleep in late next day;
later work the late-shift,
work with body, rib and spirit.
Which is when I make woman.

Making it back in

I told the man I thought his boats
the best built anywhere.

He replied
as second son of nine kids
he was destined to be boatbuilder.
The oldest took over the farm,
the younger ones went fishing.

Building boats for this sort of water
you built them tough, built boats
when they worked Cook Strait
no doubt
they'd make it back in.

It had been his job
to do just that.
He'd done just that –
no more, no less.

A matter of time and place
said the boatbuilder,
second son of the Guards,
born in French Pass.

No more, he said, no less.

Harpooner's song

Too late today to leave
I long since lost the choice.
Outside of the chase
it could be a shit of a life –
so stick it,
it never was Nantucket.

I drink, of course I drink.
It lets me think
of other lives, of anything other.
But town for me is Picton, brother,
it never was Nantucket.

The feel and the fear,
the fever of Cook Strait,
nights and mornings after
this man blown out on it.

Some days on deck sure
footed as a goat or
lucky as a drunk:
long nights, Tarwhite,
songs about harpoons
and men who made an art
of throwing them straight.

I live in Picton, brother,
but I work Cook Strait.

Too late today to leave
I long since lost the choice.
I lived for the chase.
I made the chase as art.
The town chose me
to live in it.
I chose it and called it town.

It never was Nantucket.
Picton is the town I'm in.

Floating poem

I could never work out
the difference if any
between boatbuilder and sculptor:

seen shapes float
massive as clouds
passing as the mountain

seen men in full flight
fall victim to the light
and know one thing for certain

the whole of the story
means all of them matter
as much as the other.

Like I heard silence
the first time
aboard boat

and found your loss
the first time
I knew I could float.

Fucking poem

I should write you reckon
a poem about fucking

for me I reckon that's
the hottest idea
anyone around these parts
has had in more than a year

and to Hell with the weather
or where we are
on a bed under mirrors or
arse-end of star –

psalms of dust and poetry
lost on your brown body
songs the river sings
refrains of river crossings

the song of some lost lover
who forgot there were
two sides to the river
so never crossed over.

I could I reckon
write a poem about fucking.

There isn't a river

There isn't a river
worthy the name
without rapids.

Our journey
you remind me
is a river.

You've no need
remind me
of the rapids.

That's it

Take what constellation you like,
the choice is yours.
        What you do take
will last you light years.

Step out on the jetty.
There's a slant to the inlet
        only herons see mostly.
Against me, that's it.

Naming the Gods

After the quake last night
(a rumble low in the gut
of the south Taranaki bight)
– 6.3 turns out –

I went checked his name again –
Ruamoko, Earthquake God.
Not that a man dare answer
back to a God like that.

But stand his ground if he can.
Or fall, hug in her turning,
Mother Earth;
turn with her in her pain.

While, deep beneath,
Ruamoko making life difficult
with all of these reminders
of birth and of death,

tossing them about
like they don't really matter –
everybody so mixed up a man
does not know one from the other.

A quake last night:
born again or
dead again,
doesn't really matter.

What does, what is wise to know,
is the Gods by their names.
Ruamoko is his. Pays, I think, to let him know
you know who he is.

DOUBTLESS
2008

Doubtless

When my first boy was born
I went off the road two years.
Twenty-one years on, another son,
I do the same, go off

roads, and backroads off backroads.
And if that's not enough
to keep the boys happy,
take a river of a road to the sea.

I said to the newborn
baby in my arms –

hushed, I kept it low
(didn't want to go
upsetting the olds) –

'Welcome to Death Row.'

So one man threw
his lot away
everybody knew
he'd curse the day.

Another man
thought it right
to stick with his woman
and curse the night.

He said he felt lonely
in a way he'd not known,
the thought he mightn't
make it through the night.

But he did, it seems, he's a
box of birds today
was what one nurse said.
The other looked away.

Every so often
the windbells strike
the perfect note, C sharp say.
They just did –
sure enough, C sharp!

It's said
put a monkey at a keyboard
and after so long a time –
a long, long time –
the monkey will write
a complete and
perfect work –
Shakespeare or the like.

Tonight
the windbells outside
your big bedroom windows
facing east down Lyttelton harbour

are doing just that.
They are working on Schubert's First,
and, you know, the easterly is only

just picking up.

The old man – Ngati Toa –
told me of his great uncle
stopping a bunch of settlers
drive a herd of pigs across
the Pukerua saddle.

'No Pakeha' –
with this the old man adopted
the stance of that great uncle –
'no Pakeha drives swine
across my father's backbone.'

I am the age my father
was when I was born

with crown of box-thorn
non-plussed by death

behind his left ear –
as best as I remember –

a sunset coloured feather.
That, and the nose.

I can't drive through your country
without hangover or wish to get drunk
and do it again and
again and wonder why
the foothills roll as they do,

into, out of sight,
tricks of mind, tricks of light;
how the mountains without trying to
touch the sky.

Go back to where it started
all day drinking in a far
north harbour pub; later
under a nearby boatshed
nailing a poem to that mad
old man of a grandfather.

He liked to think when he died
(which he did) his soul would stalk
the Hokianga bar
(which it does): and the Tasman
drumming, drumming on the bar.
He liked to think when he died

    these things carry on. (And they did,
    and do.) Just the way
    he wanted them to.

When I see
    trees on the skyline

I don't think
    of soldiers on parade
I don't think
    anything of soldiers I'm afraid.

When I see
    trees on the skyline
    (such as these,

        sun setting behind them)
        I know I'm not too

        far from home.
        And feel fine.

I was just about to ring you.
I forgot you were dead:

watched a programme on TV
about a new kind of rest home

they have the demented
doing the things they know

one woman baking a pavlova,
a thin man raking leaves,

somebody somewhere trying
their hardest to remember

a glimpse of last night.
Not to mention a phone number

tattoed on the arm in biro –
who? by whom?

I forgot you were dead.
I was just about to ring you.

You pointed to the rafters
said Look at the stars.

I looked for stars
but saw cobwebs.

Lady and lord,
royals of the rafters,

wrapped round the moon.
I think they made love.

The tide soon after
rose, the moon in wax.

A man had been eaten,
lord by the lady.

I looked at the cobwebs,
you mentioned clouds,

night clouds, clouds
moving north, blurring the stars.

we're all of us
daughters.

So bless his
Holy Name, Amen,

we're all of us
abandoned.

And the sun
shows no

sign of sinking and love
is not a word much

used or thought about or
practised in these parts.

We are, though,
daughters.

I set up a net,
was out after planes and highflying
migratory birds,
microphones to catch
parting words,

but ended up here –
as you see –
catching butterflies,
local atmosphere,
familiar lies.

'And I have walked on Sinbad's yellow shore'

Never knew whose
line it was

for a time, even,
thought it mine

and am no
wiser this morning,

never reckoned on
waking to this.

Sinbad's yellow shore it
may have been.

Today it's mine.
We'll share the line.

you haven't
have you

fronted as you
should the fact

you're fucked?

you've not done
any of the things

the smart couple
down the stairs do.

Like, they
know how to mix it, woman,

I mean
mix it.

Of which we know
nothing. Nor is

redemption
a word we use often.

Or have reason to.

'I like this place'
said the erudite poet
as he stepped up my stairs,
'I like it a lot!'

I told him, 'Fuck you, poet,
this place is my house.'
And I kicked him down the stairs.
With all my heart. With all of it.

Looking from 35,000
whatever they are, from a long way up,

I missed seeing your city –
that sad, flat no man's land –

I missed it completely.

You could be lost or simply
drifting off Port Levy
with the story you told at French Pass
coming to haunt you.

The truth itself
was never enough. It was something
to be built on, say, extended
as much as pocket allowed.

A bullshit artist is what
we're talking about. And a rich
one at that. God drifts by
disguised as a cloud.

Arapaoa
(to Marina Pook)

No one spells it correctly –
they weren't expected to –

and the river itself
had no say in the matter.

It was – and was for as long
as it could recall – a river.

The name came along later.
As names do, with salt rivers.

Tree poem

He stood in the middle of the field.
He thought he was a tree. He had us
believing him, as if we knew he was
more tree than man, soon to be felled.

I went out there today and spoke with him.
We spoke, shared a smoke, spoke some more.
He asked if I thought the mere
mention of his name would awaken them.

He needed to know, messianically,
if he were It! For me, I promised him
that I would follow on with word and rhyme,
my body bent beneath a fallen tree.

He was one of the last

He was one of the last
to get a taste
of the cup passed around.
When he did he made it
worth the wait;

missed what it was
the Master said –
something to do with bread
made flesh and what the
fuck was this,

wine made … ?
made Judas
just about puke. Shit,
he said I know
blood when I taste it.

Normal enough

It seemed normal enough
to nail him up

it was like he was
losing his touch

delivering sermons
most had heard before.

For the miracles –
I never saw one myself –

they won him new following
but that never lasted.

There were always new
troupes, messiahs, travellers,

hitching up or
passing through.

For me, I got there
in time for Pilate, the ditherer –

some tax man
(they reckoned a mate of Christ's)

went out and
strung himself up.

That seemed a strange one.
The rest of the time

I stuck to the pub,
heard word

they'd nailed Christ up.
I spotted it, some distance off.

At the time seemed
normal enough.

Missing you

I feel for the pulse
as well as any man
but am not out to please
so don't get me wrong:

what word I wring,
what song I sing,
ends in no Amen.
Was never meant to,

that was never the task.
I feel for the pulse
as well as any man can do
of everything, anything, that is, but you.

You are of course something else
not measured just by pulse.
Your story is incredible
your pedigree impeccable.

Which kind of
fucks it slightly –
the fact I like you,
that you quite like me.

I'm moving in closer.
Could well be a call
at 4 a.m. from the other
side of the world.

I made late love last night
a woman not half your age.
She and her friends reckoned
wrecked men are the rage.

I wasn't about, too much out of it,
to argue with that.
So when they ask where I'm at
just say I've gone to put out the cat.

And I'm not about, or out,
to say it differently.
The sun has just come up. I'm
missing you.

Snap/shot

Three books on the round table:
Buller's Birds of New Zealand
open on the tui ('both sexes sing'),
Yeat's Collected Poems – open,
'Her Praise' as would happen!
And a World Atlas a girlfriend gave me

shut as a coffin.

As we speak

Storm, nor'easter I think,
about to hit in. Right
now impossible to tell.
Everything, dead still.

Your voice faded out
the very same moment
lightning flashed and
everything went out.

Somebody said the last
drink was on the house. Whose
house it was
I never did find out.

All I knew was storm
was on its way, our way. As I'm
inclined to think it is
as we speak. This time.

Whose turn is it?

Whose turn is it
to make it into print
in the columns of the dead?

Will you come to my funeral
or will I make it to yours?

*If it's not happening now,
it soon enough will be.*

We'll wait to see, won't we,
just whose season it is, whose
name in the paper;

whose ashes it is later
catch the nor'easter.

Poem on Meg's death

Your breathing, soft now,
silences the birds.
All I hear
is a tap dripping somewhere

I know is
your heart doing its
thing at
least for the moment.

I wait outside
while family attend.
They've no need to tell me
you're gone, Meg. The tap

stopped dripping, miraculously.
And the birds started
singing like there was
no tomorrow.

I throw you flowers

I throw you flowers.

It could be a rope.
Whatever it is it's

obvious it's
worth holding onto.

As you do.
As you always did,

last one
awake in the wreck.

Patron Saint song
(for Nikki)

We talk of Anthony,
Patron Saint of Finding Things:

that holy man of Padua
only let me down
if what I'd lost
wasn't such a good idea.

I guess he, or God,
or both of them together,
decided what I'd lost
was good for me, or not.

And Christopher, P.S. of Roads and Travel,
always, somehow, got me there.

But I'm no theologian,
nor any major believer.

All I right now
do need to know –
who in Heaven the Patron Saint is
of people at the end of jetties?

Sunset song

You, you talk of the moon
cold across the mountains
the lonely and the lost
souls of albatross

battered by it all
battered by storm.
I'm staying warm now,
I'm staying warm.

Talk of things bleak
when time runs out
no wisdom, no speak
when it all points south

you lost all the magic
you lost the charm.
I'm staying warm now,
I'm staying warm.

You had all the hopes
for the future and shit
you learnt all the ropes
you knew them by heart –

what was that bit?
'if you can't stand the heat'.
I'm staying warm now,
I'm staying warm.

Prizes mean less,
victory's defeat –
you'd never guess
the ways of the cheat.

I, I'm no longer of it,
I leave it to them.
I'm staying warm now,
I'm staying warm.

No bells
(in memory, Betty Hunt)

1

What's it like?
I've seen you, mother, do
what until last Wednesday
neither had dared to.

What's it like,
did it all go dark and
that was that? Or was it all light;
and you, on this occasion, right?

2

Angels are thick on the ground,
toetoe in full bloom
down the backbone of the land:
as if our time has come –

an end to hate, to lies;
when all things change – as if to say
if the angels come this close
God can't be too far away.

3
The bamboo windbells
broke the night you died.

They were there
out on the wide verandah
doing their thing, like wind bells do,
sounding like the last of the laughter
on an Autumn evening;
the next morning, scattered,
four lengths of bamboo, empty shells.

I won't be putting them back up
out on the wide verandah,
not in a hurry.

The wind can blow
hard as it does on the Kaipara.

There'll be no bells.

What takes your fancy

What takes it, lady –
you're so different from me but we
got along

what takes your fancy
blue as the winter sea
it's bluer than blue, lady,
and lonelier than I and
lovelier than you?
Blue, so blue.

But it's okay

without you.

Cloud song
(for Eileen)

I find myself
        taking photographs
of clouds.

When I'm not
        dreaming of clouds
I wish I were

I wish I were
some other place where clouds
were the only things happening

or getting back to you
and what you would say
        you would say

the only thing on the menu
we have this evening, sir,
        is cloud.

Jimmy Vernon

Remember Jimmy Vernon,
what came of him?
Thought then of all
the boys from Hunterville,
Jimmy, Untamed Freddy and the Boys,
Heaven bent and mad as Hell.

They shacked up just out of town
in what was a farmhouse once.
When we met up in '71,
Jimmy, Untamed Freddy and the Boys,
girlfriends and kids,
were shacking in the kitchen:

a cold winter, '71, the house
good firewood! and the landlord
never had a house to call a house
to throw them out of anyway.
There was nothing to be done –
that kitchen was home.

Remember Jimmy Vernon then,
what came of him?
The barman, polishing a glass,
told me the rest:
killed on the level-crossing,
July or August last.

He nodded out the window
to the line that cuts the town in two –
the line Jimmy Vernon
crossed
but never saw the signals flash.
A cold winter, Jimmy, a good bash.

Better than this?

Parked high up Mountain Road
looking down on Point Curtis,

the one rail bridge on the Kaipara,
Ranganui;

steak pie from the
Maungaturoto bakery

FRESH! MADE TODAY!
They like their gravy
    in Maungaturoto.

And so do I,
parked up Mountain Road, high.

It doesn't get better than this.
Or so I thought

when on the Ranganui Bridge
a twin diesel and at

least two dozen wagons –
timber, mainly –

from a mile off pick up
the sound of those diesels.

How good does it get,
does it, I thought, get

better than this?

Sonata

1

There's a breeze from the south-east
collapsed on the deck.

You would never have noticed
if the doors weren't open.

You catch yourself in the mirror
close enough up to see the pores.

You don't much like what you
see, or imagine is about to happen.

2

'There's another whole
world out there!' you're

told and you, you
believe it true.

It is. No
wonder, is it, now,

or soon, soon enough,
you leave?

3
Would it not be good
(at least as a starter)

you get over the stutter
and write a sonata.

Three sections will do:
appassionata, largo and, um,

you play rhythm, Barenboim's on ivories.
I'll just hum.

Lugging the sack

The cabin boy's on deck
already up the crow's nest
yelling land out east.
We could do with some luck.

Was only last week
the same boy mistook
a herd of hump-backed whale
for uncharted atoll.

This coastline is
graveyard to sailors;
other times
refuge from storm.

If you see me
setting out to sea
enough to know I'm
hoping to make it home.

I live with my own ashes.
I buried them on a hill
underneath a cabbage tree.
They returned on the next wind.

Then I scattered them at sea
in the middle of Cook Strait
on a tide running south
too fast for any oarsman.

I made it back in and slept
the sleep of the dead. No shock,
ash in my mouth when I woke,
death in the words I spoke.

He never stopped to check
if he had a full catch
but turned and walked up the beach
leaving me to lug the sack.

He's a strange one,
Death. I never expected him
to look the way he does.
Or come when he did.

Lines for a New Year

I like the branch
I find myself on

a view over the garden
all the way down to the beach

the family below me
gathered in the garden

debating where I've gone.
My father's got a theory.

I like the branch
I find myself on.

———

You know how it is

to give up the piss
a week to the

day before Christmas

you know how it is

to fall over sober
safe in some spot,

come to later
remembering the lot.

———

the rugby ball kicked
far as the far paddock

where an apple tree caught it.
Was agreed among folk
they'd never seen such a catch,
such a kick, such a match.

———

I gave it away lately
I had no choice,
no need pump the brakes –
they'd already seized.

I like your poison, lady,
I like it too much:
which is why I am
        where I am today
outside of thought, beyond your touch.

I said I'll be seeing you.
You knew what I meant,
at least you seemed to.
Was the message you got
the same one I sent?

———

It's a love song
between a mother and son.

The son plays the drums
and wrote the song.

On the recording
mother sings the song

like mothers do. And the
son plays the drums

like a good boy. It's a
love song.

———

A friend used to say
my dog and I
had the same way of walking,

especially walking away.
Which was
often the case.

These days there's
not much happening.
It's people walking toward me

asking, where's the dog,
the dog? And they're
right. Where is he?

———

You live in this world
you have no choice.
Silence would be fine.
But you give it voice –

you have to, you cannot
help yourself.
Your mother says you never knew
when enough was enough.

———

Dreamt I met Thomas Hardy
walking a local back road.
He was an old man
but coped okay with his cane.

He said he was looking for
a woman called Lizbie Brown.
I said I knew her name –
but only from his poem.

———

Sitting on a clifftop
was always a dream
that more or less came true.
Just the words dried up.

———

Friends disappear
off the face of the earth.
For what it's worth
I loved you.
But you can't hear.

———

Is said (what few
elders we have left)
anyone for whom birds sing
all night through to dawn

are themselves
close to eternal bird-song:
their time, among these branches,
that of the elders – not long.

———

If this were the view
I got all year through –
a branch of a tree at the window –

I would become that
branch of tree and with it
grow.

The nurses agree
I never complain
about the rain, or pain.

Easy, when you know
you're a tree
at the window.

———

When I poured her a cup of tea
and asked her, strong or weak?
she held out a dark wrist:
same colour as this.

———

I'm off to look at angels.
And toetoe if I see it.

The family move in close.
No way out but

close my eyes to see

if anything's left of the toetoe,
and the angels.

———

Talking of the weather

Winter's got its teeth in
and it's going to get worse
a lot worse than this
before it gets better

before you come to, brother,
and find overnight a snowfall
lower than any local
today can recall

your dead grandmother
out on the verandah
cannot (rumour) remember
snow as low either

a lot worse than this
before it gets better
and we've not even started, brother,
talking of the weather.

CHORDS
2011

1

    I was carrying up the stairs
    a knife in a sheath,
    a bottle of wine, and two logs.
        Just thought I'd
        make a note of it.
        You know, these days
    you can't be too careful:
    good to take note
    and be a bit fearful.
    And in seventy years, say,
    when I'm well up in heaven,
    a grandkid could be asking – again –
    what was he carrying?
    And you'll be able
        to tell them the tale
        to do with firewood,
        a knife in a sheath,
        a bottle of wine
        the colour of blood.

2

You want to take a picture?

Here's my left foot.
Take one of that.

The right foot,
you want that, too?

Sorry, it's not
quite up to it,

is buried too
deep underground

to be seen, even,
let alone thought of:

a case, you could say, of
left foot, or fuck off.

3

I don't know who he is
(and don't want to)
or why you're his.
I just want you.

Walk by the ocean,
you and the dog.
I'll split the Tanian
like a totara log.

4

With age (is what they mean)
be discreet:
not right an old man
announce to the street

his love of a lady
younger than his daughter;
or be seen later, off Pahi,
walking on water.

5

All I need know

what I've got, how
long I've got?

Tell me, doctor.
Then go.

6

Good poets die young:

through love and rage
leave the song unsung.

I just hit old age.

7

This is the mound
of someone dead

an animal or child –
a child I think

the way the rocks
are mounded so –

to mark human grief
in a white-out of snow.

8

You don't have a clue
just where it is you're going to,
or where in Hell the songs come from
– would that be coming on too strong?

Your head is elsewhere
and your heart's out on hire.
They've electrified your hair
and baked you to the wire.

9

When you get God's
attention, you just somehow
know it.
        And try as you do
not to, you can't help show it.

When a man pats a dog
the world is that
much better a place. The dog
wags its tail.
        Which must mean
something, to God; and the dogs.

10 *Janáček chord*

You listen
to Janáček's Czech Requiem

and think
if God missed that

he must miss
a lot:

and keep listening
to Janáček's Czech Requiem

you think
if God only got

one chance on Earth to hear that,
we'd be a lot better off.

11

You're like the weather:

you back off now and then.
But not for long,

you're soon back,
full-on, fearsome as ever,

the usual attachments,
the power, the force.

And dressed in black
of course.

Meantime it seems
there really is

a break in the weather,
an end to lies.

But remind myself
it's only a break,

a break in the weather,
that's all it is;

find myself saying
(like, down at the shop)

I really do hope
this weather keeps up!

12

full fit of flight the swallow
picks the flicker of an eye –

your one, say, and stays well clear.
Would I'd had such radar

I would – full fit of flight –
have fucked off, oh deary-oh,

picked the flicker of an eye
for the death of all things dear.

13

That's what he called them. He'd say
"A literary verb, maybe,
but not a doing word:
it's doing nothing,

"it's not building a house
it's not crossing a river,
it's not building a bridge
or going off the edge,

"no one can follow it.
Or wants to."
I'd sometimes try to answer him.
And try making it rhyme.

Or at least do something

14

Mary the canary
just started singing.

When she starts singing
anything can happen.

Sides of mountains open,
the dead party late.

Not a good thing
when Mary starts singing.

The one you hated
more than your big sister

was all the time your lover.
And you – last to know it.

That's what Mary was singing.
Nothing could stop her.

They say the explosion
rattled cups in their saucers in Greymouth.

By that time Mary
was well past singing; or anything.

15

Why can't they speak
with words like WOOD, GOD,
WATER – words understood
that need to be heard

daily, many times,
matins at 4 a.m. –
many times in case
WATER, GOD, WOOD

or any of the rest of them –
SILENCE, STEEL, NEED –
think their names weren't said,
that their names went unheard.

Then they start getting angry
because no one sent word
that they loved them;
that they cared.

16

I wade through rhyme
push it aside like river weed,
have thoughts of open country
where verses run free

of everything, that is, but
time doing its thing.
Banks fall over. Rats climb.
Tui still sing.

I wish they wouldn't,
that they'd all fuck up!
Then I'd recite a ballad,
not so much happy, or sad,

rather, talking of the white cliffs
dropping from sight, from thought.
You never thought you'd
see them again:

but you're looking at them,
you're looking at them hard,
you're looking at them so hard
they can only stare back,

and drop if they could
from thought, from sight.

Fact is they can't.
You're the last one left.

You're out in the cold,
no rhyme to warm you:
if you're lucky a cup maybe passed
tasting of blood.

So back to the cliff top
where all you could see
was all you could see;
was all you could hold,

a bit of river weed
to slow you down, true.
No worry, friend, word
will make it through.

17

You see the faults in me
I see in you:

        there's
no way of explaining

why one moment it's stars,
the next moment raining:

nor to mention the bolts
of lightning, of thunder,
earthquake, tsunami:

the way it is,
the way it's going to be –

feeling the faults
you feel in me.

18

At high tide the orchard
was an island; low tide,
you barely notice it –
a low dune, beached on the hard.

I got back there last week,
first time in forty-nine years:
was high tide when I arrived,
the orchard out front afloat:

tried working out how many
tides would have flowed, rhymes,
how many moons, how many
deaths? Seven times seven times . . .

Around here I lose count
and falling asleep
find myself inside some
dream of a dream of a dream;

find myself turning
like the tide, too tired to turn:
but remember a bend on the Puhoi
where just about any tide

a man can make it across,
make it to the other side:
remembering, too, at full tide
the orchard is an island.

19 *Boathouse chord*

I live in a boathouse on stilts
but ponder often
the houses others live in

the mansions on the hill
where everybody gets
a private room

and corridors that go as corridors do –
adjustment time –
room to room;

or the shacks and flats
round the edge of the inlet
that look like they float.

The people who live there go
room to room –
blatblat.

I think I prefer that.

20

    Thoughts of you
make me take
    the old road north
every bridge I cross
    more water between us –

could be I'm wrong
    I quite likely am.
Rain comes on strong –
    it's not on its own.

I think of you too –
    too often.

21

Fire going on a cold
afternoon in late autumn.
Easy, growing old,
watching it all burn.

22

Is that
death on your breath?

if so
come closer – just a bit –

I like the whiff.
You were saying, death . . .

I was saying, what if?
Pure juniper.

23

How I loved you. With the sea
protesting loud but in the
end agreeing to agree –

about the time the tide
dropped away anyway, and the
whole of the night closed in –

there was everywhere to hide.
We tried them all out.
And I do it, in my mind,

again; and again . . .

24

Was I one of the twelve
who sat with you at the table?
the one still counting his beads
while the rest got stuck in.

When Judas kissed you
I thought he was on your side.
Could be I got it wrong.
Which is, it

seems, quite likely;
likely, too,
the man they nailed up
was never you.

25

When she turns she turns
ugly, leaves my ears ringing

when she burns she burns
bright as any star rising,

when she goes silent
I still hear her singing.

26

The highway under a fat moon
could be a river

with boats floating on it;
and us, in our own boat,

travelling down river to the
Dargaville wharf.

It's not a river. Of course.
But it is Dargaville.

27

Polish the monocle,
mistake it for the telescope –

either way,
see stars all day;

all night watch in hope
for first light, uncle –

you're back at sea.

28

Pure distraction.
Or song of destruction.

Until I got the words
I thought it a love song.

Good
to get it wrong,

easy to confuse
distraction for destruction,

and love for what a
fuck up it is,

and, now and then, isn't.
And words don't matter.

29

You take me to pieces, bit
by shattered bit – until I'm

left, "an image of air", no
place to go, no need to know:

just happy, falling apart,
bit by bit to the beat,

the chug of the human heart;
later, see you on the street.

30

Past noon and
nothing done
and nothing much either
likely for the afternoon:

but stare at the skyline
or near to it
as anyone gets –
stare, like you're staring it out.

Your day won't be wasted,
and nor will you. At least
not how they thought.
You'll be the focused one,

you'll be the one
they talk of, years to come.
They'll tell how you would sit,
straight-backed, staring at God.

But that's the bit
they always get wrong.
God wasn't home, back in your time –
not on your skyline.

31

Leave you to your world –
I know how rich it is.
I'm sure you'll be happy:
you'll make sure of it, I know.

Tonight the horny hound of
heaven howls. Could be tomorrow
we'll be in for snow.
You never know, do you?

32

Two o'clock and it's Tuesday.
Last night it was Monday.

I never knew you then
to be the bastard you are.

Two o'clock and Tuesday
outside of the District Court.

You can't tell these days
if you're coming or going,

if being alive is enough,
or your bruises are showing.

Two o'clock and it's Tuesday.
Wednesday tomorrow. If you're lucky.

33

His dying words, last breath:
"It is continuing, it
is continuing".

His people wondered
was it the first grandchild
born just weeks before,

was that what he meant?
Or did he mean life –
like life over death?

There has been much
discussion of such
matters round these parts.

No one seems
sure – not anymore.

34

When one of the Greats
comes in amongst us

then we – guests
eating from paper plates –

stand at the outmost circle,
thank them for calling.

We have our Gods, and Fates:
we honour them all;

when we're not out killing,
we're a humble people.

35 *Tokatoka chord*

When you make the mark,
when it's time to start dying,
time to check out the dark –
out-of-it without trying –

a time to think real estate,
land in the land of the dead;
past the barricaded gate –
trespassers prosecuted –

somewhere it's easy to park
the last, long car of them all . . .
When you hit the mark.
Or hit the wall.

And don't worry yourself,
you won't be forgotten,
you won't miss your turn
to lie flat on your back,

be carried by six
friends if you have them
in an oblong wooden box
to the top of the bluff;

be laid to rest –
six feet is enough;
like coming home,
like dust to dust.

36

Do we go over Haast then
and write a different poem?

questions I ask
especially this time of morning.

The poem may have changed
overnight

to something you couldn't handle.
Or you may have made light.

I think the latter the case:
you said the word and

light shone on the world,
on you, so beautiful.

Do we go over Haast then
and tell it all differently?

always this time of morning
questions I ask,

if overnight
the poem may have changed.

You created light –
too much of it to handle,

you said the word and
showed me your face

and said try counting to seven.
Do we go over Haast then?

37

You kept me clear of harm,
you kept harm well at bay.
How odd you seem today
not knowing even your name:

you have become, instead,
the woman you saved me from.
Which maybe's just the way
things happen when you're dead.

Do we go over Haast then?

38

I said last week
no going to work
after six-thirty;

revised it since:
six p.m. – no later –
"A Lark –

Not-an-Owl Tour",
don't want
the company of strangers,

not after dark;
by nine, able
to talk to myself

and no one over-hearing.
Then by ten,
in Heaven.

39

Remember, friend, your drive
is recorded in the dust on the bonnet
of one hot car:
would your dreams were that
easy to record; be a breeze.

Fact is it's not, now, is it?
You tumble on the shores of morning
in a bed unmade by wild seas.
Is this all you're taking,
is life worth the faking?

These are questions you wake with.
The washing-machine's on fast spin –
which kind of helps.
Is this a motel or something,
is this what life is?

– a motel built on dreams
that ended up in the suburbs,
a lowly one at that!
The woman at reception
says she's suspicious. She says

she's not quite sure of what.
She gives you an odd look.
Then you're out of there, amigo,
you're gone! your car awaits –
angle-parked, full of life's fumes:

the dust on your bonnet, you notice,
as fine as fine silk.
That's it, you've got it,
you were dreaming of dust – of
course –
and of making it there one day.

40

Letters from a friend, now dead,
piled up on the big table:
unanswered, but answerable.
But not today.

41

I used to wonder
driving the peninsula
why the feeling of dread?
learn the answer – to do
with a tribe wiped aside:

is said
if local blood shed
hadn't flowed with the tide
I'd right now be standing
waist-deep in it –

or over my head . . .
Some days later
driving a neighbouring peninsula:
the same attack,
the red tide, the panic.

42

They say soft rain is falling
in drifts across your city

where red-billed gulls and cats
gather for the frenzy.

I knew you'd be coming back –
why I waited without

complaint, or going about . . .
I knew you'd be back

gathering with the gulls and stray
cats for the frenzy:

in drifts across your city
soft rain is falling they say.

43 *All weathers chord*

My house is on the flight path
of clouds and migratory birds.
They pass through
any time, in any light,
most often so fast

I'm often left wondering
if I imagined it –
the doctor thinks it likely.
But I'm not, I know,
or don't want to think so.

So why the doors and
all of the windows
open all weathers?
So the birds, I tell you,
and clouds can pass through.

44 *Raupo chord*

I

I know I dreamt of
you last night,

this morning felt I'd
known you for years.

It's ridiculous,
I say where has

sanity gone? It went
whistling some tune out west

which is
where I

meet you in the dream,
for the first time.

II

We meet up later,
agree it's good to

see each other,
not ever admit

we're total strangers.
Where has

sanity gone? You took
me out for a meal,

there was
nothing of me left.

I know I dreamt
of you last night.

III

We can't keep on
meeting this way I

hear you
say as I come to,

keep on meeting in these
dreams as we do

it won't get us
anywhere fast,

something will break:
it will have to . . .

is what I
dreamt of you last.

IV

Whistling some tune out west,
strangers meeting at sunset

promising to remember
the whole of it tomorrow

but knowing they
won't but it

won't matter anyway.
And sanity's

long out the window . . .
Strangers then,

strangers now. And a
drowned sailor of a sunrise.

45 *The Loki chords*

I

Mother, around six last night –
night of a new moon – your first
great-grandchild was born.

Then this: at three a.m.
awake to a panic attack
that I'd forgotten to tell you.

You're years dead. I'm that many
years older: seems every so
often, though, not through death

we meet, but birth . . .
That's what I take it to mean;
and why it was a new moon.

II

Mother, the moon
was new in the sky
the night he was born.

Since then the moon
is four nights older.
As is the boy.

III

Talking late last night
(those same old dreams, I know!)

you said how amazed you were
to be a great-grandmother:

"in my own life-time" you said.
I was about to reply, Now

let's get this sorted:
I'm currently alive, and you,

if I'm right, currently dead –
said gently, not as if to

put you back in your box –
and I know it cannot be

but, mother, how is it
it was your voice that woke me?

Rain! but not enough

Rain! but not enough
to settle the dust.
I think of you often;
sometimes forget you:

forget how you ever
taught me to turn
steel to rust,
to busted trust.

But we go on
living our lives
well as we're able,
dodging the knives,

picking up whatever
falls from the table.
Rain! but not enough
to settle the dust.

A long summer

It was a long summer, and a hot one –
the hottest on record.

The people drank beer
and got fat.

When the beer ran out
they took to the wine –

first off, the whites.
Then the reds.

When the wine was cut
they took to blood,

their own, and each other's.
Some started losing weight.

Then the rains came.
And everything came right.

Blessed the fruit

I

Seems at times I sense
the mother coming through,

a sort of strangeness
I know is not you.

II

I think sometimes of this
like it's all been rehearsed:

some days it's like it is,
with most of us cursed.

III

She knew from the start
every victim by name,

knew their bitchings by heart,
shellshock suffered, the shame;

IV

why the first word was said,
was it the voice of doom?

and did it raise the dead,
the toetoe to full bloom?

V

Or was it just another
dead body dragged from the dam?

or the man she calls her brother
proclaiming I AM, I AM.

VI

You stare out the window,
and I do too:

lots of questions, I know,
answers are few.

VII

Like why the word was said,
why she left the lit room?

Answers, few. But blessed
the fruit of her womb.

Blackbird song

It's raining, and it's
going to rain, she

said, quoting Stevens I guessed.

In Stevens's case I
said to myself –

she was watching the window
like she was waiting for someone –

it was snowing. And it
was going to snow.

And didn't
a blackbird have something –

was it the song, was it
that last look on her face? –

wasn't there
a blackbird somewhere?

11 Runes (for Alf, turning 11)

1

I'm not sure what's not
or what's understood:

I'll give what I've got
to see you to manhood.

II

The sun's on the water.
It's the middle of winter.

I never had a daughter.
Or thoughts of one, either.

III

This is the way it is:
you're ten, I'm sixty-one.

These (as they say) are the facts:
we're father and son.

IV

An old friend e-mails:
says she sometimes shakes her head,

counts the miles; says she smiles,
surprised, pleased I'm not dead.

V

Nikki's right: I'm not dead,
I'm not allowed to die,

not till I'm seventy-seven, she said.
And no lie.

VI

Meantime, it's solstice,
middle of winter;

'sol in stasis',
sun low on the water.

VII

Alive, Alf, to live
clear of any city;

live as we do, five
gunshots from humanity.

VIII

Seems for the first time I'm
close enough up to tune

old words to a rhyme
to tell you the eighth rune.

IX

Three more, too, let's say
a rune a year for the kit!

Let's keep it that way
till one of us can't make it.

X

When that does happen,
I'll tell you what, Alf,

when the big doors don't open
and things fall off the shelf

XI

I'll give what I've got
to see you through,

and if I'm not
there, I'll be waiting for you.

It was the old story

I

It was the old story –
I kept hearing your voice,
I kept hearing you calling
like you were far out at sea.

For me, I was falling, falling
in love again with the story –
the old one – where we get it together
and are happy. At least in theory.

II

Another one too, remember –
they're walking up the path
and one of them falls over.
An early, small death

not ever spoken of,
not when the family gather.
They've other things on their mind –
for starters there's the weather.

Diana

I thought you a dead
princess or at least
daughter of the high priest

your name, when said,
took me some other place –
like back to the Palace! –

a different world, eh, bird,
a world where you and I
really managed to fly;

your name (in minor third)
sounding like the sound of
death – or was it love? –

I never did decide.
Names get forgotten,
the beautiful go rotten.

I thought you'd died.
But you can fly:
just watch, I hear you cry,

just watch me!

It's all okay

The washing's already
dry on the line:
I'm still as they
say doing fine:

sometimes the sea
pounds in my head.
Think of you, of me,
think of the dead.

They say what they say,
at the end of the night
you never know they
could just be right:

did I let you down or
did you fall away?
I can never remember or
know what to say.

One day I'd like to
cross paths; while we do
make love like a couple of
crazies for love:

next thing you know
it's already next day –
whatever it is it's
tearing at us –

the sun's in my eyes,
you fade away.
No lies left.
It's all okay.

They are clouds

The longer you live here
the less I'm reminded of her,
moods like clouds across sky:

they're all there today –
clouds, that is. But that is
all they are, they are clouds

I keep reminding myself.
Sometimes they stay for weeks.
Locals will say what cloudy

weather we have had lately!
And I, no longer reminded of her,
agree. Almost casually.

To a sparrow
(perched on the power-line)

unaware –
not even venturing to enquire –

of the world-
wide economic down-turn,

so unaware it
hardly seems fair.

To be a house

I

The house, without you in it,
should be condemned, too

right: there should be a law against it!
The house, to be a house, needs you.

II

Rain tonight horizontal
direct from south-west.

I never was sure, at all,
which storm-quarter was best:

III

but took to sea,
met mermaids of madness,

with the madness the beauty,
with the beauty the sadness.

IV

Your mother and I came to a bay
from some storm at sea:

what we had together was you, boy.
I never knew her, she never knew me.

V

I left on a broken down horse –
I called him 'Seven Sorrows' –

lived ten years in a lighthouse
that threw only shadows.

VI

Things change though, call it fate,
change of season, I don't know!

These nights when I ride in late
there are lights in the window.

Looking for the lights

Which way to the hospital?
There's a bell tolling –
it must be for you.

How far the furtherest hill?
I tell you what, what say
I go out there and climb it

if only to show
I've a good head for heights –
and that's before the fucking starts.

The rest can go to Hell.
Just point me home,
I'll look for the lights.

And if there's no call
it must have been the bell
ringing in your head,

tolling for you, you alone,
that woke you in tears:
old friends, dears,

reminding you they're dead.

Death notices

It more than notices –
it scrutinizes –

                until
the sun goes down
over the hill, until

the scrutinized give in.

Then Death moves on.

Last in line

You never had much of a life –
youngest of many and every
day reminded:
last in line, late for the gravy,
last in line, left for dead.
And that, not enough?

married to a man
too old to be your father.
Was like you got nothing right.
Then one day, light as a feather,
you blew away, out of all sight.
Like, so be it. Like, amen,

aamene.

KNUCKLEBONES
2012

Five knucklebones

1

You may as well not live here.
The neighbours all think you're dead

or moved to other parts.
I don't know how to tell them –

and keep my face straight – you're here,
but of late invisible.

I heard someone said they
saw you just the other day.

I told them they were lying.
I knew they knew it too . . .

You may as well not live here.
But when you do

move on, or through, let me know.
So I can start missing you.

2

This is a salt river.
And the rain heavy.
We can hardly see the river.
We can't see each other.

What life is
on the move, on a rained-out river –
you and me and salt river mist –
a lot like this.

3
I talk to you on the phone.
You're dying

you tell me, and so
alone.

As if I don't know:
I read the Book of Job today

in a Gideons Bible
in a hotel suite:

made for a light read –
with you, so alone

and your voice
going on.

I put down the phone,
 put down the good book,

found a window
open where I left it.

Then I was flying,
a mad wind had started to blow.

I didn't look.
I didn't need to.

4

I heard you'd been seen
knocking round town -
ran into Jerry and Crowd,
caught up with the Girls:

then took the Gorge
Road to the Tasman.
Where they found you,
up a gravel road

at the end of a rope.

5

"It's the zeros and ones and
twos that get us there"

was what I thought the fat nurse said.
I never will find out

what it was that
matron was about:

but thoughts keep returning
down corridors of noughts and

ones and twos and
getting nowhere.

I know it's a hospital.
That's all.

It's a hospital.
Who is

visiting who is
anybody's guess.

Cherries must be in season.
We've all got them.

Soon the visitors go home.
While the others

stay on, stay strong -
knowing they're our's,

the cherries.